GOLF
AND THE
ART OF WAR

GOLF
AND THE
ART OF WAR

How the Timeless Strategies of Sun Tzu
Can Transform Your Game

Don Wade

Thunder's Mouth Press
New York

GOLF AND THE ART OF WAR:
How the Timeless Strategies of Sun Tzu Can Transform Your Game

Published by
Thunder's Mouth Press
An imprint of Avalon Publishing Group, Inc.
245 West 17th Street, 11th floor
New York, NY 10011
www.thundersmouth.com

AVALON
publishing group incorporated

First printing, September 2006

Library of Congress Cataloging-in-Publication Data is available.

ISBN-10: 1-56025-879-9
ISBN-13: 978-1-56025-879-7

9 8 7 6 5 4 3 2 1

Book design by Maria Fernandez

Printed in the United States of America
Distributed by Publishers Group West

Contents

Introduction

*G*olf and the Art of War adopts and explains the lessons of warfare propagated by Sun Tzu's essay, *The Art of War*, and relates them to the game of golf, most precisely in the areas of strategy, competition, and course management.

The original text, which was generally believed to have been written in the fourth century BC and has been the dominant canon of Chinese—and indeed, Asian—military literature and thinking since that time. While it has been subject

to a wide variety of interpretations, its core teachings have remained remarkably constant. The *Art
of War* first came to attention in the West when it
was published in France in 1772, and quickly won
praise and adherents, not the least of whom was
Napoleon. *The Art of War* also formed the basis for
Mao Tse-tung's military and political strategies
and, to a lesser extent, those of the Soviet Union
in World War II.

Central to Sun Tzu's thesis was that careful
planning based upon sound information was the
key to a successful campaign. Among the elements he considered crucial were organization,
control, and weather. But how, specifically, does
Sun Tzu's masterpiece relate to golf? Here are but
a few examples.

Adaptability

He stresses that a successful leader must adapt to
existing situations by being flexible. He compares
this to the way that water will adapt to the contours of land. In golf, the successful player knows
when to attack a hole and when to play conservatively, much the way a military leaders assesses the
battlefield.

Dispositions

Among Sun Tzu's "dispositions" are: (1) Invincibility depends on one's self; and enemy vulnerability on him. (2) One defends when his strength is inadequate; he attacks when it is abundant. This is textbook advice for golfers who find themselves in a match-play situation.

Energy

According to Sun Tzu, "Order or disorder depends on organization; courage or cowardice on circumstances; strength or weakness dispositions." Again, in golf, this advice can help a player understand and adjust to the ebb and flow of a round.

The Five Dangers of Leadership

According to Sun Tzu, there are five potential fatal flaws that a leader (read *golfer*) must guard against. They are: reckless behavior, cowardice, a hasty temper, an exaggerated sense of honor, and an exceedingly compassionate nature.

SUN TZU'S TEN BASIC PRINCIPLES

In summary, Sun Tzu presents ten fundamental principles of warfare. Each can be related to golf in general and competition in particular.

1. Understand the potential consequences of your actions so you can plan and execute a successful strategy.
2. Play each hole for both maximum gain and minimum potential loss.
3. Eliminate your opponent at the earliest possible moment.
4. When you build a lead, strive to increase that lead, since this will allow you to increase the pressure on your opponent while reducing significant risk to yourself.
5. Do not become predictable, as this will give your opponent an advantage in knowing your thinking and possible strategy.
6. Know both your opponent and yourself.

7. When your opponent is in a weakened position, it is an opportune time to attack.

8. Don't be afraid to take a calculated gamble, but be aware of all the potential pitfalls.

9. Adapt to changing situations and momentum.

10. Golf, like warfare, is often an exercise in deception. It is good to mask your emotions and intentions.

WHO WAS SUN TZU?

S un Tzu (circa 400–330 BC) was a native of the Chinese state of Ch'i, in modern-day Shantung Province. His classic, *The Art of War*, is generally recognized as one of—if not the—earliest known compilations of military theory and strategy. Before *The Art of War* was adopted, military strategy, such as it existed at all, consisted largely of massing large armies and then setting them loose upon one another.

There is some evidence that Sun Tzu served in the King of Wu's army and there is some documentation crediting him with capturing the Ch'u capital of Ying. There is also evidence crediting him with victories in the northern Chinese states of Ch'i and Chin.

For centuries his treatise, divided into thirteen chapters, has served as the primary foundation for Chinese military strategy and has also had a strong influence on Japan and other Asian societies. In contemporary history, Chairman Mao and North Vietnam's Vo Nguyen Giap both reportedly based their strategies on Sun Tzu's teachings.

While Sun Tzu's writings are based on ancient feudal warfare and seem, at first glance, relatively simple, *The Art of War* provides a strategy for the planning and conduct of war. The two basic tenets of *The Art of War* are the preparation of adequate defenses and to seek multiple means for defeating the enemy—most importantly, ways to defeat an enemy without actually engaging him in battle. Sun Tzu argued that a thoughtful strategist could compromise an enemy without engaging it, leading to an eventual total victory.

For example, according to Sun Tzu, before entering into combat, a leader should employ tactics such as spreading rumors in the enemy camp, bribing opposing leaders, and finding other means of eroding the enemy's morale and capabilities.

Some frequently quoted axioms from *The Art of War* include: "Know the enemy, know yourself, and your victory will be inevitable," and "Avoid strength, attack weakness."

Adapting *The Art of War* to golf was not without its complications.

For starters, many of Sun Tzu's dictums, while interesting in their own right, simply had no applications for golf. For example, while it doubtlessly beneficial to forage off your enemy's territory, this seems to have little relevance to golf.

Then, there is the matter of repetition. In many instances, Sun Tzu makes the same point in several different chapters.

That said, it is fascinating to discover just how much of Sun Tzu's philosophy and how many of his teachings have applications for golf, in part because ultimately both military strategy and golf are largely cerebral pursuits.

THE ART OF WAR

by Sun Tzu
(based on the Lionel Giles translation)

CHAPTER I
Laying Plans

1. Sun Tzu said: The art of war is of vital importance to the State.

Clearly, golf is not a matter of life and death, but taking Sun Tzu's dictum with the knowledge that golf is a game, it is still one that requires the serious competitor to make every effort to maximize his advantages while minimizing his weaknesses. That said, it is useful to remember that the most successful champions are those who are able to keep competition in perspective and thus, thrive off the pressure rather than be adversely impacted by it.

One of the best examples of this came from Arnold Palmer.

One time, following a tournament, he was having a few drinks with Gardner Dickinson, a fine player who won seven times on the PGA Tour. Still, for all his success, Dickinson was frustrated that he hadn't won more often. Finally, he asked Palmer—with whom he had a 5–0 record in Ryder Cup play—what he thought was missing from Dickinson's game. Palmer carefully considered the question, and then gave an answer that provided a brilliant insight into the mind of a champion.

"I win because I love to win and I'm not afraid to lose," said Palmer. "You *need* to win and that's a big difference. You put too much pressure on yourself."

2. It is a matter of life and death, a road either to safety or to ruin. Hence it is a subject of inquiry which can on no account be neglected.

Few players ever prepared for a championship with greater diligence than Ben Hogan. Arguably the greatest example of this remarkable attention to detail came in the 1950 U.S. Open at the Merion Golf Club in the Philadelphia suburb of Ardmore.

Hogan had been seriously injured in 1949 when the car carrying he and his wife, Valerie, collided with a Greyhound bus. Hogan very nearly died, and few expected that he would be able to play golf again, let alone compete at the game's highest level. The Open at Merion would be one of his first real tests.

Despite the excruciating pain in his legs, which had borne the brunt of the damage in the collision, and his sheer exhaustion, Hogan came to the seventy-second hole needing a birdie to get into a playoff with Lloyd Mangrum and George Fazio. After a fine drive, Hogan striped a 1-iron approach to the green. Dr. Cary Middlecoff, a two-time U.S. Open champion, called it "the purest stroke I've ever seen."

Years later Hogan, with characteristic modesty, downplayed the shot.

"I had practiced that shot hundreds of times over the years," Hogan explained to a writer. "The difficult part was deciding whether to hit a 1-iron or a 4-wood."

"Excuse me," Mr. Hogan," the writer said. "Usually players carry either a 1-iron or a 4-wood. Which club did you leave out of your bag?"

"A 7-iron," Hogan said.

"Why did you leave your 7-iron out of your bag?" the writer asked.

"Because there were no 7-iron shots at Merion," Hogan said.

3. The art of war, then, is governed by five constant factors, to be taken into account in one's deliberations, when seeking to determine the conditions obtaining in the field.

4. These are: (1) The Moral Law; (2) Heaven; (3) Earth; (4) The Commander; (5) Method and Discipline.

5, 6. The Moral Law causes the people to be in complete accord with their ruler, so that they will follow him regardless of their lives, undismayed by any danger.

Much of Sun Tzu's focus is on leadership, which is perfectly understandable since his *Art of War* was written primarily for those who would dare to lead great armies into battle. While this would seem to have limited relevance to golf, it does, when you consider the importance a strong and beloved leader can have in match-play events such as the Ryder Cup, Presidents Cup, and Solheim Cup in professional golf, or the Walker Cup and Curtis Cup in amateur golf.

One of the most inspirational leaders in recent Ryder Cup history was Ben Crenshaw, who captained the U.S. team in the 1999 Matches at The Country Club in Brookline, Massachusetts.

The U.S. team entered the final day's singles play trailing the European side 10–6, meaning that Europe needed to win just four matches to retain the cup. Crenshaw, a keen student of golf history, knew all too well that teams trailing after the first two days of competition had rallied to win just three times. But he also knew that The Country Club was the place where, in 1913, Francis Ouimet, who had learned the game as a caddie at TCC, went on to upset two of the game's best players at that time, Harry Vardon and Ted Ray, to become the first native-born American to win the U.S. Open. He reminded his players that The Country Club held a magical place in American golf history, and that he was a believer in fate. He told them he had confidence in them and that he had a "good feeling" about the next day's matches.

Sure enough, they responded to their captain's confidence and, sure enough, fate intervened. In Sunday's singles play, the United States won 8½ points to Europe's 3½, and the Americans managed to win the Cup by a single point.

7. Heaven signifies night and day, cold and heat, times and seasons.

Scoring well in perfect conditions doesn't take any special talent, which is why watching Tour pros shoot fantastically low numbers in the desert, while interesting and entertaining, isn't as impressive as watching a player produce a good round in demanding weather conditions. One of the best players in these conditions is Tom Watson who, not surprisingly, won five British Opens, the major championship that generally challenges players with the most demanding combination of course design and setup, as well as weather that can change in a heartbeat.

Watson's mental strength was the primary reason he thrived in demanding conditions. While some people would let the weather beat them down and break their competitive will, and others would grind out a round by reasoning that everyone was suffering under the same conditions, Watson went them one step further. He simply reasoned that the worse the conditions, the better his chances. Therefore he looked at the physical elements of nature as something that worked to his advantage, reducing the number of players able to challenge his unique combination of athletic skills, competitive drive, and mental toughness.

RAYMOND FLOYD

FLOYD

8. Earth comprises distances, great and small; danger and security; open ground and narrow passes; the chances of life and death.

In preparing for a round, it is crucial that players study the course to determine where the dangers are greatest and where the opportunities to attack the course are most obvious. Both Ben Hogan and Jack Nicklaus, just to name two of the best players at this, were able to project what the winning score would be prior to the first shot being hit. They instinctively knew what the course would give them and where and when to attack.

One of the best examples of this came in the 1986 U.S. Open at Shinnecock Hills Golf Club in Southampton, New York. Shinnecock had hosted the second U.S. Open (and U.S. Amateur) in 1896.

Raymond Floyd came to the Open playing well, but curiously for a player who had won a Masters Tournament and two PGA Championships, he had a relatively poor record in the U.S. Open—in part because the way the United States Golf Association grew the rough around the greens negated one of the greatest strengths of his considerable game—his chipping and pitching.

But in the course of playing his practice rounds,

Floyd came up with a game plan. He carefully plotted where he had to play conservatively, and where, if the conditions were right, he could afford to take a risk and gamble.

Despite four days of temptations, Floyd stuck to his plan religiously, never wavering. In the final round, in very difficult conditions, he carved out a 66 to edge Lanny Wadkins and Chip Beck by two strokes.

"I made up my game plan and never wavered from it," said an emotional Floyd following his win. "I trusted it and stayed with it."

9. The Commander stands for the virtues of wisdom, sincerity, benevolence, courage, and strictness.

It should be obvious that the game's greatest champions share a wealth of similar characteristics, not the least of which are a keen intelligence and a mental and physical discipline, two hallmarks of successful commanders according to Sun Tzu. Success at the highest levels of the game simply isn't possible with sloppy or careless thinking or behavior. That said, another quality the game's greatest champions seem to share is simply that they genuinely like themselves. For example, did anyone every enjoy being themselves more than Arnold Palmer? It's doubtful.

One person who made this observation quite publicly is Australia's five-time British Open champion, Peter Thomson.

In 1993, Thomson was in St. Andrews watching the Dunhill Cup competition being played at the Old Course. He was sitting in his room in the Old Course Hotel, being interviewed by a reporter. The room offered views of the sixteenth and seventeenth holes.

In the course of the interview, he and the writer observed John Daly hit a beautiful, soft approach into the sixteenth green and then watched him blister a drive on the par-4 seventeenth, the infamous "Road Hole."

"That man has as much talent as anyone who has ever played the game, and when I say that I'm including Sam Snead and Seve Ballesteros," said Thomson. "Of course, the pity is that he so clearly dislikes himself and for that reason, he will never fully realize the fruits of his remarkable skills. You cannot succeed in this game if you don't like yourself."

Sad to say, but as Daly's record has proven,

Thomson was prescient. While Daly has won five times coming into the 2006 PGA Tour season (including a PGA Championship and the 1995 British Open at the Old Course), no honest assessment of his career would indicate he's even come close to realizing his remarkable potential.

And Thomson was also right when he said that it is a pity.

10. By method and discipline are to be understood the marshaling of the army in its proper subdivisions, the graduations of rank among the officers, the maintenance of roads by which supplies may reach the army, and the control of military expenditure.

Again, when applied to golf, this observation from Sun Tzu would apply to players who come fully prepared to the first tee. They know any local rules; have the proper equipment for the course situation (taking care to make sure they have the proper number of clubs); items like bandages, sun block, snack items, a sufficient number of golf balls, gloves, etc., foul weather clothing, and so on. It is another common denominator to successful players that they are meticulously organized, leaving as little as possible to chance.

Consider if you will, the case of Wales's Ian Woosnam at a recent British Open. Entering the final round with an excellent chance of winning, when he reached the second tee, his caddie—who was horrified by his discovery—told Woosnam that there was an extra driver in the bag, a one-stroke-per-hole penalty.

Woosnam, who was understandably shaken, finished in a tie for third place.

Does anyone think something like that would ever happen to Jack Nicklaus?

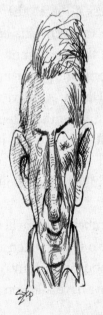

11. These five heads should be familiar to every general: he who knows them will be victorious; he who knows them not will fail.

Therefore, as Sun Tzu suggests, when looking at young players entering the professional tours, one way to accurately predict which individuals are likely to enjoy the greatest success is to assess which have the most—or indeed all—of the qualities described in *The Art of War* as they apply to championship golf. As has become increasingly obvious, simply having a wealth of talent is no guarantee of success if these other valuable qualities are lacking in a player. This brings to mind a classic story about the late Tommy Armour.

Armour was a brilliant player in the era of Bob Jones and Walter Hagen. A native of Scotland, he won a U.S. Open, a British Open, and a PGA Championship. At the end of his competitive career, he gained considerable notoriety as a teacher at the Winged Foot Golf Club outside New York City.

One day a member approached Armour and asked him to come out and watch a young man he was planning to sponsor on Tour play a few holes. Since Armour didn't have a lesson or a card game at the moment (in reverse order of importance to Armour), he went out and watched the kid play a few holes—during which the young man had a hard time keeping the ball on the course, let alone the fairways. After a respectable period of time, Armour excused himself and headed back to the clubhouse, where he doubtlessly had two gins waiting for him—the card game and a gin buck, a drink he particularly favored. A short time later, the member approached Armour.

"Tommy, I'm very sorry," he said. "He was just nervous playing in front of you. He does have a beautiful swing, doesn't he?"

"Yes, it's magnificent," said Armour. "The problem is it doesn't work."

12. Therefore, in your deliberations, when seeking to determine the military conditions, let them be made the basis of a comparison, in this way:

13. (1) Which of the two sovereigns is imbued with the Moral Law? (2) Which of the two generals has most ability? (3) With whom lie the advantages derived from Heaven and Earth? (4)

On which side is discipline most rigorously enforced? (5) Which army is stronger? (6) On which side are officers and men more highly trained? (7) In which army is there the greater constancy both in reward and punishment?

14. By means of these seven considerations I can forecast victory or defeat.

Dave Marr, the 1965 PGA Champion who went on to enjoy a much-acclaimed career as a golf analyst for ABC, NBC, and the BBC, was kind and generous with his advice to young writers just starting their careers. When asked which players he thought had the best chances for victory at the start of a tournament, he divided the field into different groups, much the way Sun Tzu thought he could forecast victory or defeat.

"First, you look at the guys whose games suit the course," he said. "For example, at Augusta National, you look for guys who can hit the ball high and have a great touch around the greens. That's why Jack [Nicklaus] is so good there. He can just launch those beautiful, soft approach shots, even with his long irons. He doesn't have to fool around with spin, because he has the advantage of height. Lee Trevino is a low-ball hitter, so Augusta is a tough course for him. But put him on a course where the wind blows and you have to work the ball, and he'll kill you. Look at some of the courses where he won majors: Oak Hill, Merion, Royal Birkdale, and Muirfield—all courses where you better have your A game when it comes to shot-making.

"Second, look at the record books and see who has had success on this particular course," Marr said. "There are just some courses that fit your eye and you feel comfortable there. That gives a guy a little extra confidence.

"Next, you look at the guys who have been successful coming into the tournament," Marr went on. "That means they're playing well and have a little bit of extra confidence in the games. That's sometimes just enough to give you an edge.

"Finally, you always go with the heroes, because they can win any time and on any course," he concluded. "I mean, in their primes would you ever bet against Arnold [Palmer] or Jack? Are you kidding?"

26

15. The general that hearkens to my counsel and acts upon it, will conquer: let such a one be retained in command! The general that hearkens not to my counsel nor acts upon it will suffer defeat: let such a one be dismissed!

In the final round of the 1974 U.S. Open at Winged Foot, a young Tom Watson, finding himself in contention on a brutally difficult course, struggled mightily and eventually fell back, opening the door for Hale Irwin, who went on to win his first of three Opens.

Many writers and commentators blamed Watson's collapse on his "choking," but Byron Nelson, who was working as an analyst for ABC at the Open, knew better. As one of the game's greatest champions, he knew all too well the pressures of competition at the highest levels of the game.

When play ended, Nelson sought out Watson in the locker room. The two men spoke for a while, and Nelson, also one of the game's finest gentlemen, told Watson that if he ever wanted to talk or have Nelson work with him on his game, he should just call.

"I was very touched by how kind and thoughtful Byron was, but being stubborn, it took me a while to take him up on his offer," Watson explained. "I practiced with him many times and we developed a wonderful friendship. He looked at my swing but his greatest influence was on the mental aspects of the game. In terms of my swing, he just tweaked it here and there. He is a great cheerleader. He always stressed what was good about my swing and my game and never focused on what was bad. He's just an incredibly positive person. In the end, what he really gave me that was most important was confidence."

16. While heeding the profit of my counsel, avail yourself also of any helpful circumstances over and beyond the ordinary rules.

In golf, as in warfare or competition of any sort, the reality is the contest or battle is fluid and, thus, constantly changing. It is rarely, if ever, static. With that in mind, it is crucial that participants remain alert to any change in the situation, or circumstances, as Sun Tzu refers to it.

A textbook example of adjusting your game and your mental approach owing to the changing conditions came in the final round of the 1996 Masters, when England's Nick Faldo made up a six-stroke deficit to catch and then surpass Australia's Greg Norman to win by five strokes.

Faldo, who had already won two Masters, began his planning for the final round after his round on Saturday.

"I began by reminding myself that I could catch Greg," Faldo explained. "I thought if I could cut his lead to three strokes after the front nine, well then, lots have guys have blown three-shot leads on the back nine at Augusta National."

Norman, who when he was firing on all cylinders, was one of the longest, straightest drivers of the ball the game had ever seen, began his final round ominously, hitting his tee shot through the fairway and into the trees guarding the left side of the first hole.

"He's blocked by the trees, so I'm thinking here's my chance to pick up at least one stroke on him," said Faldo, who did just that when Norman failed to get up and down from a greenside bunker.

"Standing on the second tee, I noticed that Greg began gripping and regripping his club," said Faldo. "I thought that was something different, since usually with Greg he always went through the same pre-shot routine. He'd shuffle his feet a couple times, grip and regrip, and then go.

Norman came back with a birdie on the par-5 second hole, as did Faldo. Norman managed to get up and down to save par on the short, par-4 third hole and then made a bogey on the par-3 fourth hole when he aggressively shot at the front-right hole location, ended up in the bunker, and made bogey. Coming to the sixth hole, a dangerous downhill par-3, Norman had a five-stroke lead. But sensing an opening, Faldo attacked from the tee, knocking his tee ball four feet from the hole and making a birdie to cut the lead to four strokes.

It looked as though Norman had righted the ship on the seventh hole, when he ripped a sand wedge six feet from the hole. But just as he had on two previous putts, he pulled his putt and had to settle for par.

On the uphill, par-5 eighth, Norman hit a monstrous drive and decided to gamble and try to hit the green in two with a 3-wood. Again, Faldo noticed that Norman seemed uncomfortable over the ball, which rested on an uphill lie. When he finally pulled the trigger, his shot rocketed to the left, ending up in the trees. He made a fine recovery for par, but lost a stroke as the conservative Faldo laid back short of the green, hit an indifferent third shot with a wedge, but holed a twenty-footer for birdie to cut Norman's lead to three—just what Faldo had been hoping for as he mentally prepared for the round.

On the par-4 ninth hole, Norman made a fatal error—if not in planning, then at least in execution. With the hole cut in its traditional Sunday, front placement, Norman hit a sand wedge from one hundred yards, and then watched in disbelief as the ball landed on the putting surface and spun back off the green, leaving him with an extremely difficult pitch back up the hill. Had he hit his approach just one yard longer, he might well have made a birdie. Instead, despite a valiant pitch, he had to settle for par, shooting a 38 on the outward nine.

What happened in the holes that followed literally reduced grown men to tears.

Ben Crenshaw, working as a commentator for CBS Sports in the Butler Cabin studio, excused himself, went outside to the small patio, and cried. Nick Price, one of Norman's closest friends on Tour, was watching the telecast in the clubhouse. As Norman's collapse continued unabated he left. It was simply too painful to watch.

A poor approach on ten, followed by an equally bad chip, led to a bogey, as did three putts on the par-4 eleventh. Now Faldo changed his mindset.

"Greg made a series of unforced errors," Faldo recalled. "On ten, he had a straightforward 8-iron and pulled it. Then he jammed the chip and missed the putt. I thought then that he was really in trouble. After he three-putted eleven, we were tied and I couldn't fathom how he could have crumbled so badly in such a small space of time. What happened on the ninth hole was a mistake where he'd come up just short. It really wasn't that bad a shot. But after ten, I realized it was really getting to him. The tenth was the result of bad shots."

There would be more to follow.

Clearly shaken as he stood on the tee of the dangerous, par-3 twelfth, Norman inexplicably decided to attack one of the most dangerous hole locations on the course. Instead of playing safe and targeting his tee ball over the bunker guarding the front of the putting surface, he went at the pin which was cut to the right side of the green. His 7-iron landed on the green, jumped forward, and then began its inexorable roll back off the green and into the water hazard. The best Norman could do was make a double bogey, and after Faldo made his fourth straight par, he had a two-stroke lead.

Given Norman's length and the fact that there are two very reachable par-5s on the back nine, Faldo's two-stroke lead was far from insurmountable, but on the first of those hole—the thirteenth—Norman's distracted thought process was laid out for the world to see.

Norman's drive landed atop the pine straw, and

while he had just 213 yards to carry the creek and reach the green, the straw made it a risky play—and this was time to stop the bleeding, not open another vein.

"I think I can get there with a 2-iron," he told his caddie, Tony Navarro.

"We don't have to make everything back on one hole," Navarro gently suggested.

"Can I get there with a 2-iron?" Norman asked.

"I think you can, but I wonder if that's a good play or not," Navarro insisted. "I just don't think that's the play. I think we can lay up and make a four."

Norman wasn't persuaded.

"I want to hit the 2-iron,' he said. "That's what I want to do."

"If you think that's the right play, then let's go for it," said Navarro, trying to be as supportive as possible.

In the end, Norman had an epiphany of sorts, laid up, pitched to within ten feet, and finally made a putt for birdie.

On the par-5 fifteenth, Norman's 6-iron approach came up short, but it left him with a relatively easy chip (easy, except for all that had gone before it). He hit a brilliant chip that barely missed going in for an eagle. Moments later, Faldo hit a fine third shot of his own.

"If Greg had made his and I had missed, we would have been tied again," said Faldo. "I hit a great little bump-and-run to about three feet. It was a very hard shot because anything could have happened. I could have left it at my feet or run it ten feet past the hole."

"I had an easier shot than Nick, and if it had gone in we would have had a whole new ball game," said Norman. "That's why I put so much into it and why it was so hard for me to regroup and go on."

In the end, he couldn't.

Norman's tee shot on the par-3 sixteenth found the pond guarding the putting surface and he made a double bogey and Faldo went on to win by a remarkable five strokes.

"To me, that final round was the best mental commitment I've ever had," said Faldo. "I had to walk through every shot, whereas before it had always happened spontaneously. I knew what to do and how to do it and I just pushed myself through the process."

17. Accordingly, as circumstances are favorable, one should modify one's plans.

In golf, as in any form of competition, momentum is important but it is also fluid, shifting from one competitor to his opponent. It is the wise competitor who, as Sun Tzu suggests, alters his strategy accordingly.

In the final round of the 1986 Masters, forty-six-year-old Jack Nicklaus was poised to do the unthinkable: win his record sixth Green Jacket. After opening with rounds of 74–71–69 and turning the front side in 35, he could sense that momentum was building in his favor.

Standing in the fairway on the downhill, par-5 fifteenth, he studied his second shot and asked his son, Jackie, who was his caddie, "How far do you think a 3 will go here?"

"Pretty far," said Jackie.

Nicklaus, one of the greatest long-iron players in history, launched a towering 4-iron from 212 yards out. The ball covered the flagstick all the way and came to rest twelve feet from the hole, leaving him a good putt for an eagle. As he did so often in his remarkable career, Nicklaus made the putt and then headed for the tee on the par-3 sixteenth.

Nicklaus's tee shot had barely left the clubface when Jackie said, "Be good."

"It is," said Nicklaus.

Nicklaus made a birdie on sixteen and now with the complete support of the enormous gallery, made another birdie on the par-4 seventeenth. After making a par on the eighteenth hole for a score of 30 on the inward nine, all he could do was wait and see if his lead would hold up.

When both Greg Norman and Tom Kite came up short in their bids to tie him, Nicklaus had pulled off another miracle.

Conversely, when the circumstances are unfavorable, a player should adjust his strategy and thinking accordingly, witness this story about Ben Hogan.

One year, while playing in the U.S. Open, Joe Dey, the executive director of the United States Golf Association, approached Hogan before his round and urged him to pick up his pace of play. Implied in his statement was the not-so-subtle threat that if Hogan didn't play faster, he might be penalized.

"Joe, if you're planning to put one [stroke] on me, tell me now so I can plan for it," said Hogan.

No penalty was levied. It wasn't necessary.

18. All warfare is based on deception.

There is a considerable consensus of opinion which holds that Billy Casper might be the most underrated of all the game's great players. Casper won fifty-one PGA Tour events including the 1970 Masters and the U.S. Open in 1959 and 1966, and also won nine Champions Tour titles, including the 1983 U.S. Senior Open.

Perhaps Casper's most remarkable victory was in the 1966 U.S. Open at San Francisco's Olympic Club, when he caught Arnold Palmer in the final round and went on to beat him in a playoff the following day. What made Casper's win so amazing was that it was almost totally unexpected—by everyone except Casper himself.

After the first two rounds, Casper and Palmer were tied but Casper struggled with his driver on Saturday, and at the end of the day he'd shot a 73 and trailed Palmer by three strokes.

On Sunday, Palmer blistered the front nine in 32, and took a seemingly insurmountable seven-stroke lead into the final nine. As they made the turn, Casper told Palmer that it looked like he (Casper) was playing for second place.

"Well, if there's anything I can do to help you, let me know," said Palmer.

This attitude, coupled with Palmer's determination to break Ben Hogan's Open record of 276, would sow the seed for Palmer's collapse.

For years, people have debated whether Casper was practicing a very subtle gamesmanship with his comment to Palmer. If he was, he was acting out Sun Tzu's dictum about deception.

Palmer bogeyed numbers ten and thirteen but still had a five-stroke lead with five holes to play. But on the 150-yard, par-3 fifteenth, Palmer elected to attack the hole rather than play safely. His tee ball ended up in a bunker and he wound up making another bogey, while the methodical Casper hit the green safely and ran in long putt to cut the lead to three strokes.

Like a fog rolling in off the nearby Pacific, a sense of impending doom began to settle over the enormous, largely pro-Palmer gallery. For three-and-a-half rounds, Palmer's instinctive aggressiveness had brought him to the brink of his second U.S. Open title. Now, the question became, could it become his undoing?

The thought occurred to Palmer.

"Suddenly, it dawned on me that Billy Casper had a chance to the tournament," he observed. "But, to me, it didn't look like a very good chance. The sixteenth was a long par 5 and it was not an easy birdie hole and neither was the seventeenth. The eighteenth was a short par 4, so he might get a birdie there, but I couldn't imagine he'd make three straight birdies."

As it turned out, he didn't need to.

Instead of playing safely and hitting a 1-iron into play from the tee on the sixteenth hole, Palmer pulled out his driver.

"I thought how it would look: 'There goes Palmer, playing it safe with a 1-iron when he's got a three-stroke lead with three holes left to play.'

"In the end, I couldn't do it," he went on. "I had to be aggressive and play the hole the way I feel it, not the way somebody else might play it. I decided to go for broke."

Palmer's drive smashed into the trees and dropped straight down into Olympic's formidable rough. In and of itself, this wouldn't have been the end of the world. It was his next shot that pretty much proved to be. Instead of taking a lofted club and pitching the ball back into the fairway, he tried to reach the green with a 3-iron, an almost impossible shot, even for a player with Palmer's strength. The ball carried a mere seventy-five yards, remaining in the rough.

"I was surprised when I saw Arnold take a long iron but nothing he does really surprises me," said Casper, who could scarcely believe his eyes. "When he's playing well, he believes he can do anything."

When the dust had settled, Palmer made a 6 and Casper made a 4, cutting the lead to a previously unthinkable, single stroke.

By now, Palmer was in a full meltdown. On the seventeenth, he missed a six-footer for par and fell into a tie with Casper. On the home hole, he scrambled brilliantly to save par and must have breathed an enormous sigh of relief when Casper— one of the game's greatest putters, barely missed his fourteen-footer for birdie.

The next day's playoff was eerily reminiscent of the previous day's play. Palmer led by two strokes after the front nine, but shot a 40 on the inward nine to lose by four strokes.

It was a loss many people believe Palmer never truly recovered from.

In a considerably less dramatic fashion, perhaps the greatest story about deception concerns a money match between Dr. Cary Middlecoff and Doug Sanders, a player whose considerable skills were generally overshadowed by his kaleidoscopic wardrobe and equally colorful personality.

"When I was nineteen or twenty, I used to play at a club called La Gorce, which was in Hollywood,

Florida," Sanders recalled. "There were more big-money games up there than you could shake a stick at and Doc was a regular. At that time, Doc has the most unbelievable caddie in the world. In the days before everyone played by yardage, you went by what your eyes told you and this guy was phenomenal. He'd tell exactly what club to hit and how to hit it. He might say, 'Hit a 5-iron and take off three yards', or 'Hit a 7 and add two yards.' He knew Doc's game inside and out and Doc trusted him completely. He was the best caddie I ever saw.

"Well, one day I had a big match lined up with Doc, so I went to this guy at La Gorce and paid him a few bucks to fix some of the pins. He shortened some and added a little length to others, and then he replaced a few of the regular pins with the ones he'd doctored. If a hole was cut on the front of the green, just over a bunker, he'd put the long pin in the cup, so the shot would look shorter than it actually was. As a result, Doc was in bunkers all day. If a hole was cut towards the back of a green, he'd put in a longer pin and Doc's ball would still be rising as it went over the green. It wasn't long before the caddie was completely confused and Doc was getting all over his back.

"Twenty years later, I ran into the caddie and he told me that was the worst day he ever had," Sanders continued.

"'Doug, I've never been that bad at judging distances in my whole life,'" he said. "'I don't know what the hell was going on. I gave Doc the wrong club every time.'"

"You should have seen his expression when I told him what happened," said Sanders.

19. Hence, when able to attack, we must seem unable; when using our forces, we must seem inactive; when we are near, we must make the enemy believe we are far away; when far away, we must make him believe we are near.

While players like Arnold Palmer, Lanny Wadkins, and Tiger Woods wear their emotions on their sleeves, Sun Tzu's lesson dictates a less emotional approach to competition. He seems to indicate that the optimum approach is one where you mask your intentions as well as your emotions.

An excellent example of a player who has this approach is Tom Watson, who goes about his business on the course with a stoic determination. If he hits a bad shot or has a bad break, he simply moves on to the next shot. This emotional resolve might help explain why he is so effective in bad weather. It also is one reason he has enjoyed so much success in the British Open, which he has won five times.

"When I first went over to Scotland and Ireland and played the great links courses, I really didn't like them," Watson says. "I learned to play the game through the air and not along the ground. It took a long time for me to accept the bad bounces that are a part of the game. But after a while, that style of play grew on me and I became fascinated by it. To play on links courses, you need to have patience and a certain equilibrium. If you don't, you won't have much success."

20. Hold out baits to entice the enemy. Feign disorder and crush him.

Walter Hagen was a master of match play and head-to-head competition, in no small part because he was a keen observer of human nature.

One time, when Sam Snead was just coming out on Tour, he faced Hagen in a match. When they reached one of the first par-3s on the course, Hagen had the honor. As he deliberated over what club it hit, he noticed that the young Snead was taking more than a casual interest in Hagen's club selection. That helped Hagen make up his mind.

"This hole plays longer than it appears," he said to his caddie, making sure he said it loud enough for Snead to hear him. "I think it's the 5-iron."

With that, Hagen pulled out the 5-iron but "dead-handed" the shot, hitting it about the distance of a 6-iron. The ball ended up pin high.

Suitably impressed, Snead pulled out his 5-iron and hit it beautifully—a touch too beautifully, as it turned out. The ball was still rising when it flew over the spectators behind the green.

"Sonny," said Hagen to Snead as they walked off the tee. "You're playing with the big boys now. Don't ever go to school on what club a man pulls from his bag."

Another splendid example of Hagen at his best (or worst depending on your point of view) came in the 1927 PGA Championship at Cedar Crest Country Club in Dallas.

Hagen met Joe Turnesa in the final and the gamesmanship began early. Turnesa warmed up and then waited anxiously on the first tee for Hagen, who casually arrived a half hour late (on occasion, Hagen would arrive in a tuxedo, explaining that he'd been at a party all night and simply lost track of the time) and apologized profusely to Turnesa.

Without bothering to so much as hit a practice putt, Hagen proceeded to tank the first three holes of the match, spotting Turnesa a three-up lead.

"There, Joe," Hagen said. "That makes up for the half hour you had to wait. Now we'll play."

Hagen managed to eat into Turnesa's lead and by the time they reached the final hole, the match was all square. But on the home hole, Hagen hit a poor drive and faced an approach from thick grass to a green blocked by a stand of tall trees. As Turnesa watched helplessly from the middle of the fairway (he should have known better by this time) Hagen went into his routine. This included shaking his head in despair, walking back and forth to the green, checking the wind, changing clubs, consulting with his caddie, commiserating with the gallery, and every other trick he could think of. Finally, he announced (loudly enough for Turnesa to hear) that he might have to take an unplayable lie. This brought groans and protests from the fiercely pro-Hagen gallery. Finally, Hagen announced that he'd try to reach the green but it would require a "miracle shot." Naturally, there was nothing miraculous about it, and Hagen's approach ended up twelve feet from the hole.

By this time, Turnesa's thought process was scrambled and his confidence completely shaken. He dumped his approach shot into a bunker, failed to get up-and-down, and lost, one-up.

21. If he is secure at all points, be prepared for him. If he is in superior strength, evade him.

This doesn't apply so much to an opponent as it does to the golf course itself. On any top-quality course, there are simply holes that you cannot attack, or, if you do so, run the risk of running up a very big number in a hurry. The key is recognizing which holes those are and planning your strategy accordingly. It also applies to how you play individual holes. Most well-designed holes will give you a place where you can minimize the penalties for a miss.

A classic example of this is the West Course at Winged Foot Golf Club, the site of numerous national championships including, most recently, the 2006 U.S. Open. The key to scoring well at Winged Foot is "keeping the course in front of you." In other words, the greens that A. W. Tillinghast designed are so beautifully and strategically bunkered that missing them to the sides leaves a far more difficult recovery than if you come up short of the putting surface.

A case in point was the way Billy Casper played the 213-yard, par-3 third hole en route to his victory in the 1959 U.S. Open. The tee shot required a long iron to a difficult target. Casper, who had a brilliant short game, elected to play short of the putting surface each day. It proved to be a wise strategy, as he made four straight pars.

After the tournament, Casper ran into Ben Hogan, who paid him a compliment—of sorts.

"If you couldn't putt, you'd be selling hot dogs out here," Hogan said.

22. If your opponent is of choleric temper, seek to irritate him. Pretend to be weak, that he may grow arrogant.

Spain's Seve Ballesteros, whose nine PGA Tour victories include three wins in the British Open and two Masters titles, was an absolute genius, particularly when it came to escaping from trouble. To this day, his fellow players still tell stories of his derring-do.

It is fair to say that Ballesteros was the heart and soul of the European Ryder Cup team. His charisma and sheer audaciousness inspired his teammates to a string of victories beginning with their first-ever win on American soil, in the 1987 Matches at Muirfield Village Golf Club.

Ballesteros was particularly effective in match-play situations, in part because he was a keen judge of human nature and also because he had such immense talent that he could intimidate his opponents. Not to accuse him of gamesmanship, but members of the U.S. team would privately cite Seve's tendency to cough, sneeze, or clear his throat at opportune (or inopportune, depending on your point of view) moments in a match. Whether or not this was intentional or the result of allergies (as he insisted), it did tend to be a particularly effective diversion against high-strung or nervous opponents.

Of course, this sort of stuff works better in some cases than in others. Sometimes it backfires completely, witness the story of a memorable run-in between Sam Snead and Lloyd Mangrum.

Mangrum, a member of the World Golf Hall of Fame, won thirty-six PGA Tour events including the 1946 U.S. Open. He also had a much-deserved reputation as one tough guy.

"One of the few run-ins I ever had with another player was with Lloyd," recalled Snead. "I knew he had a reputation for gamesmanship and so I was kind of on guard when we were paired in the final group on the last day of a tournament. Right from the first tee, every time I teed it up he'd move in real close to me and then just as I'd start my swing he'd move, trying to distract me. I kept my mouth shut for as long as I could and then finally I'd seen enough. When he did it again I stepped away from my ball and walked right over to him.

"'Lloyd, you've been trying to throw me off all day. All I want is a fair chance. Now give me a little room,' I said, and he knew I was ready to mix it up with him right then and there, if it came to that.

"There was a big gallery around the tee, and they cheered. This one old bird said, 'Atta boy, Sam. He's been after you all day.'

"Lloyd never bothered me again," Sam said.

23. If he is taking his ease, give him no rest. If his forces are united, separate them.

It is generally conceded that if a fast player is paired with a slow player, it is the fast player who will suffer, because his sense of pace and timing will frequently be thrown off. But in a match-play situation, a player can help even the odds by walking quickly between shots.

"Jack Nicklaus took a lot of time once he reached his ball, because he was very methodical," Lee Trevino often observed. "But between shots he'd walk you to death. He didn't do it on purpose. It was just his way of keeping up with the pace of play."

24. Attack him where he is unprepared, appear where you are not expected.

Throughout his remarkable career, Tiger Woods

has pulled off any number of shots that bordered on the unbelievable, but surely one of the greatest came in the 2000 Bell Canadian Open at the Glen Abbey Golf Club near Toronto.

Playing the final hole of the championship, Woods hit a poor drive that found a fairway bunker. The drive left him with 218 yards to the hole, but it required him to carry the large lake that protected the front of the putting surface. After watching Grant Waite hit his approach some thirty feet from the hole, Woods, who had a one-stroke lead, had to decide whether to lay up or gamble and shoot at the hole. It didn't take long for him to make a decision. He pulled out a 6-iron and hit it perfectly. The ball soared over the water and came to rest in the fringe, fifteen feet from the hole. Moments later, he secured his victory, his third national championship of the season, after winning both the U.S. Open and the British Open.

"Obviously, that was the shot that won the tournament for him," said Waite. "To have that mindset, that poise, that calmness inside his body to be able to make that swing and to hit that shot just shows you that he's got such an enormous advantage over the rest of the players.

"Tiger is an incredible man who is playing golf like nobody in the universe has ever played it," Waite added. "Maybe out there in some other universe some guy can do this, but in this one, where we are, nobody has ever stepped into a pair of golf shoes and played the game like this."

25. These military devices, leading to victory, must not be divulged beforehand.

Almost no one ever goes into a round announcing their plans, short of saying they are going to try and "hit fairways and greens." For one thing, golf is such a fluid game that even the most carefully conceived game plan is subject to change for any variety of reasons.

But the real strategy, as Sun Tzu refers to it in this dictum, seems to be directed to team competitions, where captains try to figure out which players they will pair together—or when they will send a player out in singles play—with an eye to what he or she thinks the opposing captain will do.

An excellent example of this is in the final day's singles play. Is it a wiser strategy to send your strongest players out first, in order to build momentum, or save them for the latter stages of the day, when the pressure may well be greatest—all the while realizing that your opponent is making the same calculations?

26. Now the general who wins a battle makes many calculations in his temple where the battle is fought. The general who loses a battle makes but few calculations beforehand. Thus do many calculations lead to victory and few calculations to defeat: how much more no calculation at all! It is by attention to this point that I can foresee who is likely to win or lose.

Peter Thomson, the brilliant Australian who won five British Opens, understood all too well this lesson from Sun Tzu.

In the earlier decades of the twentieth century, practice as we think of it today was virtually an alien concept. Players might hit a few balls to warm up before a round, or hit a few more afterwards to work out some problem in their swing. But spend hours on a practice tee or green? Rarely, if ever.

For his part, Thomson preferred spending his time and energy on the course in the days prior to the start of play.

"It's stupid to rely upon the mechanical theory that what you did on the practice ground will repeat automatically on the course," he said. "The circumstances are entirely different. The view from the tee must affect you. Suddenly there are bunkers and out-of-bounds to think about. My purpose in playing a practice round is to learn where the serious trouble is and to get the pace of the course to determine how the ball is bouncing."

CHAPTER II

Waging War

1. Sun Tzu said: In the operations of war, where there are in the field a thousand swift chariots, as many heavy chariots, and a hundred thousand mail-clad soldiers, with provisions enough to carry them a thousand Li, the expenditure at home and at the front, including entertainment of guests, small items such as glue and paint, and sums spent on chariots and armor, will reach the total of a thousand ounces of silver per day. Such is the cost of raising an army of 100,000 men.

2. When you engage in actual fighting, if victory is long in coming, then men's weapons will grow dull and their ardor will be damped. If you lay siege to a town, you will exhaust your strength.

The best example of this truism in recent years has been the phenomenal record Tiger Woods has amassed when pushed into extra holes, either in match-play events such as the U.S. Amateur (which he won three times) or the World Golf Championships-Accenture Match Play Championship (where he has two victories) or at the 2000 PGA Championship where he beat Bob May in a playoff, which is, in effect, a match-play situation. On top of all that, coming into the 2006 PGA Tour season, his playoff record is an astonishing 8–1.

It is a remarkable commentary on both his golf skills and mental toughness that when his back is up against the wall, he seems to concentrate more clearly and raise his performance to the level required for victory. This a rarity, since a great percentage of golfers tend to suffer a letdown when pressed into extra holes or when they find they must rally to keep a match alive.

Why is this? As Sun Tzu suggests, it may simply be the natural reaction to an extended battle, and only the strongest, best prepared, and mentally toughest can elevate their performances to the required levels.

3. Again, if the campaign is protracted, the resources of the State will not be equal to the strain.

It is a historical oddity that for all his greatness, Ben Hogan was not particularly successful in play-offs. One theory holds that he was so intensely focused upon the job at hand—winning a seventy-two-hole, stroke-play event—that he was simply spent by the physical and mental effort.

"He [Hogan] would pick a target score for a game plan and never deviate," observed two-time Masters champion Ben Crenshaw. "He wouldn't just outshoot the field, he'd outthink the world."

Perhaps his most surprising playoff loss came in the 1995 U.S. Open at San Francisco's Olympic Club.

Hogan appeared to have his fifth Open title locked up. Indeed, he had already given the ball he putted out on the seventy-second hole to Joseph C. Dey, the executive director of the United States Golf Association.

"Here Joe," he said. "This is for Golf House."

The only player left on the course who could catch Hogan was Jack Fleck, a pro at a driving range in Iowa. As unlikely as it seemed, Fleck did just that, setting up an eighteenth-hole playoff the following day.

When writers asked Hogan about Fleck, Hogan replied simply, "He must be a good player. He plays Hogan clubs."

Later, to a small group of friends, Hogan's

comments spoke volumes about how drained and exhausted he was.

"I wish he had made a 2 on the last hole," said Hogan, his voice barely audible.

In the playoff, Hogan's right foot slipped on the downswing as he drove on the home hole, resulting in a hooked drive that ended in the thick rough that lines the hillside along the left side of the hole. In the end, he made a thirty-footer, but it didn't really matter. It was for pride as much as anything else. He lost by three strokes.

Later, Tommy Armour, a winner of the U.S. and British Opens and the PGA Championship, observed that the playoff had simply taken too great an emotional toll on Hogan.

"His foot didn't slip," said Armour. "His heart did."

4. Now, when your weapons are dulled, your ardor damped, your strength exhausted and your treasure spent, other chieftains will spring up to take advantage of your extremity. Then no man, however wise, will be able to avert the consequences that must ensue.

One of the finest and most historic examples of this lesson from Sun Tzu came in the playoff between Sam Snead and Ben Hogan in the 1954 Masters—the tournament that Bobby Jones called the finest Masters he'd ever seen.

Snead and Hogan were the two dominant players of that time and this was particularly true when it came to the Masters. Snead had won in 1949 and 1952 while Hogan took home the Green Jacket in 1951 and 1953.

The two men—who along with Byron Nelson were known as the "Great American Triumvirate"— were fierce rivals who always seemed to elevate their games when facing each other.

The two tied after seventy-two holes, setting up an eighteen-hole playoff for the following day. As they stood on the first tee, Snead asked Hogan if he wanted to split the first-and-second-place purses, a practice that was not uncommon at that time. He did this in part to protect his financial interest (no small consideration given the size of the purses in those days), but also as a way to judge how confident Hogan was feeling. (It is important to remember here that Hogan had nearly been killed in a 1949 automobile accident and still suffered from pain and weakness in his legs, which were severely injured in the crash).

"Ben took a couple of long drags from his cigarette, put those steely blues on me (his eyes), and said, 'Let's play.'" Snead recalled years later.

Apparently there was nothing wrong with Hogan's confidence level . . . or if there was, he wasn't going to give any hints to Snead.

The two were tied at one-under par-35 at the turn, but Snead won the 10th when he chipped in from sixty-five feet. He gave up the lead with a bogey on the treacherous, par-3 twelfth and then regained it with a birdie on the par-5 thirteenth. After the two made pars on numbers fourteen and fifteen, they came to the par-3 sixteenth and what proved to be the turning point in the playoff.

"The hole was cut in a place where you couldn't really attack it so I decided that with a one-shot lead, I'd play safe," Snead recalled. "I hit it in there to about twenty-five feet and Ben put it inside me, about eighteen feet from the hole.

"Now, I knew Ben's mannerisms about as well as anyone," Snead continued. "Ben used to deal cards in a casino when he went broke out on Tour in the early days, so he was pretty good about hiding his emotions, but while I was lining up my putt I noticed that Ben was really dragging hard on his cigarette. The more I watched him, the more nervous he seemed to me. I knew that after four rounds of regulation play, his legs must have been hurting him and he had to be getting tired, so I decided I'd take a real good run at my putt. I had a stroke to play with and thought that if I could turn up the heat on him, I might just put him away right then and there. My putt ran a foot past the hole, and I just decided to sit back and see what Ben would do.

"Well, damned if he didn't hit one of the worst putts I ever saw him hit," said Snead. "His putter hit behind the ball and he left it five feet short. When he missed that one, I said to myself, 'Well, Sambo, lookie here.'"

Snead went on to win by a stroke, 70-71.

5. Thus, though we have heard of stupid haste in war, cleverness has never been seen associated with long delays.

Indecision often results in a lack of confidence and poor results. Think of your own game: if you're like most people, when you are playing your best you're on a kind of cruise control. You see the shot or the putt and react instinctively. On the other hand, when you see players taking a long time deliberating over a shot, the results are generally poor. This is especially true for putting. As a general rule, your first instinct is almost always correct. Very often, for example, players who read a putt from both behind the ball and from the other side of the hole, only manage to get mixed signals. If you have trouble reading putts, try reading them from behind the ball only. You might be pleased with the results.

6. There is no instance of a country having benefited from prolonged warfare.

True, and by the same token, no one benefits from a prolonged match, especially if you're in a tournament and face a second match later in the day. If at all possible, close out your match as quickly as possible, even if this means taking a chance or two if it might give you the edge. Very often, a defensive strategy only prolongs the match.

7. It is only one who is thoroughly acquainted with the evils of war that can thoroughly understand the profitable way of carrying it on.

Ah, this brings us to the heart of a debate that has been ongoing for the past thirty or so years on the professional tours.

As teaching professionals have become more skilled (and more skillful at self-promotion!) and received greater attention in the media, playing professionals on all the tours have sought out their advice—not to mention help from sports psychologists, health and nutrition experts, and others.

Not surprisingly, players from earlier generations have greeted this development with skepticism, if not outright scorn. For them, the best way to learn—both a swing and how to win—lay in Ben Hogan's famous dictum: "The secret is out there; you just have to dig it out of the dirt."

Lee Trevino was even more to the point.

"I'd never take a lesson from a guy who couldn't beat me," he has often famously stated.

Now, clearly this only applies to a very small percentage of the world's golfers—those that compete on the highest levels, either as amateurs or professionals, but it is an interesting question. Can a person who has never experienced the excruciating pressure of tournament competition fully and properly teach someone who hopes to?

Sun Tzu would argue not.

8. The skillful soldier does not raise a second levy, neither are his supply-wagons loaded more than twice.

When playing a money match, it's a good idea to keep in mind the old poker saying, "You've got to know when to hold 'em, know when to fold 'em." A good example is this story about a match between Sam Snead, Billy Farrell, and Raymond Floyd.

"We were in Greensboro for the tournament and I was going to play a practice round with Billy Farrell, Johnny Farrell's son, who had been a fine player for a long time," Snead recalled. "Raymond Floyd had just come out on Tour and while I didn't know him, I'd heard that he had a lot of confidence in his game and wasn't opposed to backing it up with a little action. Now, I won Greensboro eight times, so you might say I was pretty comfortable on the course. But I got off to a bad start and both Billy and Raymond had me down at the turn. I offered to double the bets on the back.

"I think I'll pass," said Billy.

"Raymond said he'd take all of me he could get—which is pretty much what he got," Snead continued. "I shot a 28 on the back nine and walked away quietly."

9. Bring war material with you from home, but forage on the enemy. Thus the army will have food enough for its needs.

10. Poverty of the State exchequer causes an army to be maintained by contributions from a distance. Contributing to maintain an army at a distance causes the people to be impoverished.

11. On the other hand, the proximity of an army causes prices to go up; and high prices cause the people's substance to be drained away.

12. When their substance is drained away, the peasantry will be afflicted by heavy exactions.

13, 14. With this loss of substance and exhaustion of strength, the homes of the people will be stripped bare, and three-tenths of their income will be dissipated; while government expenses for broken chariots, worn-out horses, breast-plates and helmets, bows and arrows, spears and shields, protective mantles, draught-oxen and heavy wagons, will amount to four-tenths of its total revenue.

15. Hence a wise general makes a point of foraging on the enemy. One cartload of the enemy's provisions is equivalent to twenty of one's own, and likewise a single picul of his provender is equivalent to twenty from one's own store.

16. Now in order to kill the enemy, our men must be roused to anger; that there may be advantage from defeating the enemy, they must have their rewards.

The rewards that come with victory are fairly obvious, but the larger question here is Sun Tzu's contention that a warrior must be roused to anger to be most effective.

Two-time U.S. Open champion Curtis Strange is an excellent case in point. A ferocious competitor who won seventeen times on the PGA Tour, Strange has always claimed that he played his best when he was able to work up a nice, hot bit of anger against an opponent, particularly in match play.

"That's one reason I was never very good against Jay Haas (a college teammate at Wake Forest University)," said Strange. "He's such a nice guy I couldn't think of anything to get mad at him about."

Stories about Jack Nicklaus becoming angry on a golf course are few and far between, but Tom Weiskopf has a classic.

"Jack and I used to play a lot of our practice rounds together," says Weiskopf, who has known Nicklaus since their days at Ohio State University. "At Carnoustie in 1975, we went out after dinner, which was fairly common since it stays light for so long there at that time of year. We were on the second green when we heard [Australian] Jack Newton [who would lose that year's British Open in a playoff with Tom Watson] and [Irish professional] John O'Leary yelling to us from the tee. When they caught up with us, Newton said they wanted to challenge us to a match. I was pretty sure Nicklaus wasn't interested, because in practice rounds he never focused on shooting a score but was just trying to figure out how to fit his game to how the course was playing that week.

"Now you have to remember that even though it was in the evening, there was probably a gallery of several hundred people watching us," Weiskopf continued. "Newton kept badgering Jack and me, saying stuff like 'You're supposed to be the two best players in the world but you're afraid to play us,' and so on. On the third hole, Newton made a birdie and then he ran in a forty-footer for another birdie on number 5. After he made his putt, he was kind of gloating and he looked over at Jack and asked if we wanted a press. Now remember, at this point, we hadn't even agreed to a match but Newton's attitude really burned Jack. He gave Newton a look I don't think I've ever seen, either before or since. He just burned him with those icy blues. He said, 'Jack, we're not two-down yet.' With that, he ran in a ten-footer for a half.

"Well, all of a sudden, the game was on," Weiskopf continues. "We agreed to ten-dollar automatic one-downs. On the sixth tee, Jack took me aside, looked me right in the eyes, and said, 'Tom, if you've ever tried in your life, I want you to really try now. I want to bury these guys.' He was scary.

"In all the years I've known Jack and competed against him, I've never seen him as intense as he was that night," says Weiskopf. "Between us, we made twelve birdies and an eagle and just massacred Newton and O'Leary."

Despite displaying flashes of a considerable temper early in his career, Bobby Jones was a model competitor for most of his years. Like Jack Nicklaus, who idolized Jones, he was a fierce but instinctively gracious competitor. There was, however, one occasion when he took an active dislike to an opponent and vowed to beat him as badly as he possible could.

"He came up to me before the final round of a championship," Jones once told a close friend, without identifying either the player or the championship. "He told me that he really didn't care which one of us won, that he just wanted to have a pleasant round and hoped that the best man would win. I didn't like that. I knew he wanted to win very much—just as much as I did—and he wasn't being honest with me. I wanted to beat him very badly from that moment on."

17. Therefore in chariot fighting, when ten or more chariots have been taken, those should be rewarded who took the first. Our own flags should be substituted for those of the enemy, and the chariots mingled and used in conjunction with ours. The captured soldiers should be kindly treated and kept.

It is interesting to watch the captains in a team competition such as the Ryder Cup, Presidents Cup, Solheim Cup, or amateur competitions such as the Walker Cup or the Curtis Cup, particularly in the final day's singles play.

Almost to a person, they make a point of being

out on the course as a match finishes, to either congratulate their player or commiserate with them. The players who have finished their matches generally remain on the course to offer support for their teammates.

This sense of teamwork reflects the spirit Sun Tzu referred to in the above passage.

18. This is called using the conquered foe to augment one's own strength.

Again, as in the above passage, the idea is to use momentum to your advantage whenever possible. If you are playing in a team event, and your opponent sees your teammates' joy and enthusiasm and, at the same time, his teammates' frustration and disappointment, this can be very beneficial. Again, a perfect case in point is how momentum changed so dramatically to the United States's side in the 1999 Ryder Cup Matches at The Country Club. When the Americans ran off a string of victories in the early singles play on the final day, the Europeans became dispirited while the U.S. players in the latter matches were energized.

19. In war, then, let your great object be victory, not lengthy campaigns.

Of all the game's truly great players, the only one that comes to mind that violated this dictum was JoAnne Gunderson Carner or, as she was known during her amateur career, the "Great Gundy."

As an amateur, Carner won the 1956 U.S. Girls'

Junior and five U.S. Women's Amateurs. She is also the last amateur to win an LPGA event. As a professional, she won forty-three LPGA titles including two U.S. Women's Opens.

Carner was a joyful warrior and the game's history is replete with stories about her facing a clearly inferior opponent in match play and carrying her along in a match, just because she enjoyed the competition and the companionship and took no particular pleasure in watching an opponent suffer a humiliating defeat.

Of course, it didn't hurt that she was such a dominant player that there was rarely a risk of her letting a match get out of hand.

20. Thus it may be known that the leader of armies is the arbiter of the people's fate, the man on whom it depends whether the nation shall be in peace or in peril.

On the face of it, this dictum from Sun Tzu does not seem to have much to do with golf, per se. However, if you look at it in the context of a team, match-play event, you can see that the influence of a strong and respected captain on his players can be profound. Take the 1965 Ryder

Cup Matches at Royal Birkdale Golf Club in Southport, England.

Byron Nelson captained the U.S. team and while he was deeply respected by all his players, he was beloved by Ken Venturi, who Nelson had mentored early in his career.

Venturi, who had won the U.S. Open in 1964, came to Birkdale suffering from circulatory problems in his hands that would eventually end his playing career. In fact, the problem was so severe at Birkdale that on several occasions he had to wear gloves to keep his hands warm.

The Matches were hard fought, but surely one turning point came in an alternate shot match between Venutri and his partner, Tony Lema, and Neil Coles and Brian Barnes.

On one of the final holes, Lema hooked his second shot, leaving Venturi with a delicate pitch off a downhill lie, over a bunker, to a pin cut just past the hazard.

"I'm afraid things don't look very good for your side," Prime Minister Harold Wilson said to Nelson. "I don't favor your man's chances with this shot. I believe the match may go even here."

"That may be, Mr. Wilson," Nelson said. "But if

I had to pick one of my men to play this shot for me, it's the man playing the shot right now."

Venturi's pitch ended stiff to the hole for a birdie.

"My, Mr. Nelson," said Wilson. "You do know your men, don't you?"

CHAPTER III

Attack by Stratagem

1. Sun Tzu said: In the practical art of war, the best thing of all is to take the enemy's country whole and intact; to shatter and destroy it is not so good. So, too, it is better to recapture an army entire than to destroy it, to capture a regiment, a detachment or a company entire than to destroy them.

2. Hence to fight and conquer in all your battles is not supreme excellence; supreme excellence consists in breaking the enemy's resistance without fighting.

When you think of "supreme excellence" in golf, the first name that should come to mind is Jack Nicklaus. With that in mind, Sun Tzu is right on the money.

Nicklaus was supremely confident even as a teenager, winning two U.S. Amateurs and finishing second in the 1960 U.S. Open as a twenty-year-old. Indeed, his performance in the final thirty-six holes (the Open played thirty-six holes on Saturday until 1965) prompted Ben Hogan to tell the press, "I played with a kid today who should have won this tournament by ten strokes." Tom Weiskopf, Nicklaus's teammate at Ohio State, went Hogan one better: "Jack was already the best player in the world when he was in college."

Nicklaus has always been the very picture of sportsmanship, humble in victory and gracious in defeat.

"Jack Nicklaus is a great winner and an even better loser," his longtime friend and rival Gary Player has often observed.

In truth, Nicklaus was so dominant that, in many cases, he had gone a long way to victory before the first ball was ever hit in a championship.

"Jack knew he was going to beat you," said Lee Trevino, who offered one of the most spirited challenges to Nicklaus both on the PGA Tour and on the Champions Tour. "He knew he was going to beat you. You knew he was going to beat you. And he knew you knew he was going to beat you."

As a lot of very, very good players discovered over the decades, that was an awfully high burden to overcome.

3. Thus the highest form of generalship is to balk the enemy's plans; the next best is to prevent the

junction of the enemy's forces; the next in order is to attack the enemy's army in the field; and the worst policy of all is to besiege walled cities.

This applies nicely to course strategy. First, avoid falling into any strategic traps devised by the architect. Realize that the design may be such that it will lull you into making a mistake. Next, identify the holes that can be attacked if the conditions are favorable, which might be worth a gamble, and which require you to settle for a par and move on.

One year at the Masters Tournament, Bobby Jones was listening to some players at the champions' dinner complain about how difficult it was to make birdies on some of the holes. Finally, Jones had heard enough.

"I don't agree with that and, frankly, don't understand it," said Jones. "If you apply the proper imagination and strike the ball properly, you might get close enough to reasonably expect to make a birdie. That is all the course owes you."

4. The rule is, not to besiege walled cities if it can possibly be avoided. The preparation of movable shelters, and various implements of war, will take up three whole months; and the

piling up of mounds over against the walls will take three months more.

5. The general, unable to control his irritation, will launch his men to the assault like swarming ants, with the result that one-third of his men are slain, while the town still remains untaken. Such are the disastrous effects of a siege.

Sam Snead used to describe his mental approach as being "cool-mad."

"You don't want to lose your temper, because then you can't think clearly," Snead said. "But you just have to have the attitude that you want to stomp the other guy into the ground. If I've got a guy two-down, I want to get him three-down and in a hurry. I don't care if it's my brother or my best friend, that's my attitude."

6. Therefore the skillful leader subdues the enemy's troops without any fighting; he captures their cities without laying siege to them; he overthrows their kingdom without lengthy operations in the field.

Sun Tzu seems to be talking about the power of intimidation in this dictum. Historically, while there have been many players who could dominate in their era, there are few that were so superior that they could intimidate the field. One was Bobby Jones.

Jones competed as an amateur but dominated pros and amateurs alike, a reality that infuriated Walter Hagen, the consummate professional.

"You guys make me sick," he once said to a group of his fellow professionals. "Jones enters the tournament and you give up. None of you think he can be beaten. Well, I think he can be beaten and I think I'm just the one to do it."

But in truth, Jones really *was* just that dominant.

"Hagen would get angry with his fellow professionals because they were intimidated by Bob," said two-time PGA champion Paul Runyan, a contemporary of Jones and Hagen. "To a degree, that was quite true. But Bob was just that much better than everyone else. When he and I would play a friendly match, he would give me a stroke a side and I will be very candid with you and admit that I probably needed more than that. I had to play extremely well to beat Bob, even with the strokes.

"Tommy Armour had a similar arrangement," Runyan continued. "Bob would spot him a hole at the start of each nine. In other words, Tommy would begin each nine one-up. When a writer asked Armour, who had tremendous pride, why he would agree to such an arrangement, he said that it was because Bobby was just that good."

7. With his forces intact he will dispute the mastery of the Empire, and thus, without losing a man, his triumph will be complete. This is the method of attacking by stratagem.

8. It is the rule in war, if our forces are ten to the enemy's one, to surround him; if five to one, to attack him; if twice as numerous, to divide our army into two.

9. If equally matched, we can offer battle; if slightly inferior in numbers, we can avoid the enemy; if quite unequal in every way, we can flee from him.

When Sam Snead came out on Tour in 1937 few, if any, of the established players had heard much about him. After all, he had grown up in Virginia's Blue Ridge Mountains and had only played in events around the state. At one of his first tournaments, he got an education into life on Tour.

"I arrived a few days early and was looking for someone to play a practice round with," Snead said. "I ran into Dutch Harrison and Bob Hamilton and I asked if I could join them. They agreed and asked if I wanted to have a little wager. I wasn't much on gambling but I wanted to get along with them, so I agreed.

"Well, I hit my first two drives out into the boonies on the first hole and I just knew they thought they had found a real pigeon," he continued. "Hell, I wasn't too sure they hadn't, but pretty soon I settled down and began matching them shot for shot.

"After a while, I was getting the better of them and Dutch tried to give me the needle about my so-called strong grip.

"'Young man, you've got a fine swing there,' Dutch said. 'That hook grip doesn't seem to bother you at all.'

"I'd heard all that before, so I just ignored him and tried a bit harder," Snead said. "By the end of the day, I'd won a little money from those boys and told them I sure would like to like to play them again the next day.

"'Sonny,' Dutch said. 'You work your side of the street and we'll work ours.'"

• • •

A similar story involving Sam Snead was often told by the legendary teacher, Harvey Penick, who taught Ben Crenshaw and Tom Kite, among numerous other top players.

"I was playing in the Houston Open one year and all the players were talking about this fellow from the mountains of Virginia," Penick said. "They said they'd never seen anyone who could hit the ball quite like him. One of the players said that he'd played with Sam a few weeks earlier and he generated so much power that the sleeves tore away from his shirt at the shoulders. I went over to see for myself and they weren't exaggerating. Not only had I never seen a ball hit like that, but I'd never heard a shot sound like it did when Sam hit it. It came off the clubface with a crack, like a rifle shot. At that moment, I decided that the life of a teaching professional looked pretty good to me."

10. Hence, though an obstinate fight may be made by a small force, in the end it must be captured by the larger force.

It may well be that golf fans, more than people who follow other sports, understand this and pull for the dominant players and against the underdogs. Take the case of the 2000 PGA Championship at the Valhalla Golf Club.

Tiger Woods met Bob May in a three-hole playoff. The two had been friends and rivals since their junior golf days in southern California, where May was a dominant player. While Woods went on to achieve enormous success, May struggled, in part due to injuries.

While a victory by May would have been a wonderful Cinderella story, it is the nature of the game that the vast majority of the people in the gallery—and, in truth, the pressroom—were pulling for a Woods victory.

Indeed, you can take this one step further and look at the history of the four U.S. Opens played at San Francisco's Olympic Club.

In 1955, Jack Fleck beat Ben Hogan.

In 1966, Billy Casper beat Arnold Palmer.

In 1987, Scott Simpson beat Tom Watson.

And in 1998, Lee Janzen beat another gallery favorite, Payne Stewart.

Little wonder than that the Olympic Club is known among writers as the club where the wrong guy always wins.

11. Now the general is the bulwark of the State; if the bulwark is complete at all points; the State will be strong; if the bulwark is defective, the State will be weak.

Lee Trevino takes justifiable pride in his work ethic but insists he worked as hard as he did because he had no other choice.

"I'm self-taught," he said. "No one ever taught me how to play. I did it in the back alleys, the back of driving ranges, out in the fields. Wherever I could hit balls, that's where you'd find me, but for a long time it was never on courses. I learned to play golf in a completely different way and I probably spent more time at it than anyone else. I had to, because I didn't have anyone to teach me the proper fundamentals. When you have bad fundamentals, then you have to spend three times longer learning the game than a player who had good fundaments right from the start. Harvey Penick put it perfectly when he said that if you have a good grip, you don't have to work as hard as a player with a bad grip."

12. There are three ways in which a ruler can bring misfortune upon his army:

13. (1) By commanding the army to advance or to retreat, being ignorant of the fact that it cannot obey. This is called hobbling the army.

14. (2) By attempting to govern an army in the same way as he administers a kingdom, being ignorant of the conditions which obtain in an army. This causes restlessness in the soldier's minds.

15. (3) By employing the officers of his army without discrimination, through ignorance of the military principle of adaptation to circumstances. This shakes the confidence of the soldiers.

16. But when the army is restless and distrustful, trouble is sure to come from the other feudal princes. This is simply bringing anarchy into the army, and flinging victory away.

17. Thus we may know that there are five essentials for victory: (1) He will win who knows when to fight and when not to fight. (2) He will win who knows how to handle both superior and inferior forces. (3) He will win whose army is animated by the same spirit throughout all its ranks. (4) He will win who, prepared himself, waits to take the enemy unprepared. (5) He will win who has military capacity and is not interfered with by the sovereign.

18. Hence the saying: If you know the enemy and know yourself, you need not fear the result of a hundred battles. If you know yourself but not the enemy, for every victory gained you will also

suffer a defeat. If you know neither the enemy nor yourself, you will succumb in every battle.

This dictum from Sun Tzu seems particularly appropriate as it pertains to match play competitions.

A player who knows himself knows his strengths as well as his weaknesses. For example, following his second consecutive U.S. Open victory, Curtis Strange talked about his qualities as a player.

"I'm not sure I can ever be a dominant player," Strange said. "I can get my share of wins, but if you look at the players who dominated—Nicklaus, Palmer, Snead, Hogan, guys like that, one thing they all had in common is that they were really strong. That helps if you hit the ball in the rough and it really helps in bad weather. I just don't have the physical strength that they had. Now, my biggest strength is that I don't kid myself. I know what I can do and what I can't do and so I try to play within myself. I also don't make a lot of dumb mistakes. Sure, I hit bad shots, but everyone does. That's just the nature of the game. But I don't think I make many bad decisions, and that's a big difference.

"The other thing is I perform pretty well under pressure," he continues. "I'm like the basketball player who always wants to take the last shot with the game on the line. I have that kind of confidence because I've usually been successful under that kind of pressure, going back to when I was a kid. In that respect, I think success breeds success."

Just as Strange has enjoyed considerable success in match play, so, too, did his fellow Virginian Sam Snead.

"I played all the sports growing up and you learn to watch your opponent and learn what makes them tick," Snead said. "You study their mannerisms. Most players change their routines under pressure. I always tried to stay in mine, because I didn't want to tip my hand. When I was playing the Tour pretty regularly, I could go into the locker room and look at the shoes lined up in front of the lockers and tell you whose locker it was just by the shoes. That's how closely I studied the other guys."

Snead also made a point of playing within himself.

"Unless the hole called for a draw, I'd generally try and hit a nice little fade off the tee," Snead explained. "I just felt that gave me a little better control. I was playing with J. C. [his nephew, J. C. Snead, who also enjoyed success on the PGA Tour and Champions Tour] in the 1978 PGA Championship at Oakland

Hills. We got up on the tee and he tried to give me the needle by asking me if I was 'going to hit that crappy little fade again.' I said, 'Well, I would like to get it in the fairway, which you haven't been doing too often today.' I think he got the message."

CHAPTER IV
Tactical Dispositions

1. Sun Tzu said: The good fighters of old first put themselves beyond the possibility of defeat, and then waited for an opportunity of defeating the enemy.

Jack Nicklaus was the perfect example of this dictum. When playing in a tournament, especially a major championship, he would play fairly conservative golf, especially in the early rounds. Now certainly, if the opportunity to attack the course presented itself, he would make the most of it, but as a general rule, he would get himself either in or near the lead in the final round and then wait for others to make mistakes. He understood that while he enjoyed pressure—reveled in it, actually—it was destructive for most of his opponents (save the handful who gave him his greatest challenges) and would almost inevitably cause them to make mistakes, either in thinking or execution, as the final round went on.

2. To secure ourselves against defeat lies in our own hands, but the opportunity of defeating the enemy is provided by the enemy himself.

Again, if there is one truism about golf, it is that the successful player is the one who is best able to minimize his mistakes. Generally, two-time U.S. Open champion Curtis Strange was a master at this. He played within himself and was a very mentally tough competitor. But in one famous case—the final round of the 1985 Masters—he made a mistake that was completely out of character.

Strange opened with an 80 and seemed all but certain to miss the cut. But he fought back and by the time he reached the par-5 thirteenth hole, he held a two-stroke lead. But after his tee shot, Strange faced a difficult decision. His drive was good enough that he could try and hit the green in two, but it was a risky shot. When he elected to gamble, Ken Venturi, who had two second-place finishes in the Masters and was covering the hole for CBS, spoke ominously about Strange's chances.

"He's bringing 6 and maybe a 7 into play here," Venturi said.

Strange's shot came up short and into the water, as did his approach on the next par-5, the fifteenth hole. He wound up tied for second with Seve Ballesteros and Raymond Floyd, one stroke behind Germany's Bernhard Langer.

3. Thus the good fighter is able to secure himself against defeat, but cannot make certain of defeating the enemy.

In the final analysis, all you can do is play your own game. Certainly, a wise player is one that knows where his opposition stands, but focusing too intently on the rest of the field can easily become a distraction.

4. Hence the saying: One may know how to conquer without being able to do it.

In other words, beware of the perils that come with overconfidence. Very often, when facing a superior player, a decided underdog will elevate his game. This is because, in part, since he is not expected to prevail, there is a decided lack of pressure on him. It is for this reason that Bob Jones and other top players dread the early rounds of match-play competitions. There are too many strange twists, lucky breaks, and bad bounces that can contribute to an upset. Take the case of Jack Nicklaus in the 1975 Ryder Cup Matches at Laurel Valley Country Club.

While the U.S. team went on to win yet another lopsided victory against the team from Great Britain and Ireland, this time 21–11, the big story was England's Brian Barnes, who beat Nicklaus twice in back-to-back singles matches on the final day. He beat the game's dominant player, 4–2, in the morning match and then, in an even more unlikely victory, beat Nicklaus, 2–1, in the afternoon. This in spite of the fact that Nicklaus, his pride bruised, was determined to avenge his morning loss, as Barnes recalled years after the competition.

"I still, after all these years, have difficulty in

getting away from it," Barnes said. "Whenever I attend a company day or dinner, I am introduced as the man who twice beat Jack Nicklaus head-to-head. But you know, I never did consider it as that fantastic. Certainly I enjoyed it at the time, but in my own mind I soon forgot it.

"Eighteen holes of match play is not a lot different from a sudden-death playoff, and two wins like that do not mean as much to a professional as they would to an amateur.

"I do know how bloody mad Jack was, but he never showed it and congratulated me very warmly," Barnes continued. "We talked a lot about fishing in the morning match and, you know, Jack was responsible for seeing that we played again in the afternoon. America had won the cup by then and it was he that went to [U.S. team captain] Arnold Palmer and suggested that the order of play should be fiddled with so that we met again. It gave the crowd something to look forward to watching. I remember Jack saying to me on the first tee: 'You've beaten me once but there ain't no way you're going to beat me again.' Then he started birdie, birdie, birdie and I didn't think I would, but somehow I did."

5. Security against defeat implies defensive tactics; ability to defeat the enemy means taking the offensive.

In 1956, Ken Venturi was one of the finest amateur golfers in the country and figured to become the heir to Byron Nelson (his mentor) and Ben Hogan (a friend) when and if he turned professional. He was a confident, stylish player and an intense competitor, and it really wasn't surprising that he was leading going into the final round of the 1956 Masters Tournament. The twenty-four-year old had led after each of the preceding three rounds.

On the eve of the final round, Clifford Roberts, the cofounder and chairman of the Augusta National Golf Club told Venturi that he thought it would be best if he wasn't paired with Nelson in the final round, which was one of the tournament's traditions. Roberts feared that if Venturi should win while playing with his dear friend and mentor, it might tarnish his victory. Instead, he told Venturi he could play with anyone else of his choosing. Venturi, with the supreme confidence of youth, asked to be paired with Sam Snead.

"I wanted to come up the eighteenth fairway with a great player," he'd say later.

Sunday's round proved to be extremely challenging, to say the least. The wind howled, drying out the course and making the greens nearly impossible to putt. Venturi, trying desperately to hold on to his lead, made a critical mistake in strategy by playing defensively.

"I made the mistake of trying to two-putt, which is the easiest way to three-putt," Venturi has said many times. "It started on nine when I missed a short putt and bogeyed the hole. I was hitting the greens but having trouble putting. The greens were as hard as concrete and very bumpy."

Venturi wasn't alone is his struggles that day. Twenty-eight other players failed to break 80 and only two, Snead and Jack Burke, managed to break par. Burke's one-under-par 71 was good enough to edge Venturi, who shot an 80, by a stroke.

"Its funny how fate has a way of stepping into your life," Venturi says. "If I had won the Masters I probably would never have turned pro and might not have ever won the [U.S.] Open."

6. Standing on the defensive indicates insufficient strength; attacking, a superabundance of strength.

One of the marks of a great champion is being able to take a lead, no matter how large or small, and hold it in a final round. Tiger Woods is superb at this, being virtually unbeatable when he has the lead going into the final round. A member of the World Golf Hall of Fame that was a great front-runner was Dr. Cary Middlecoff, who won thirty-seven PGA Tour events including two U.S. Opens and the 1955 Masters.

"Doc was a tough man to catch once he had a lead," recalled Sam Snead. "He was like a race-horse that was ready to go once he got the bit in his mouth. Doc was fearless when he got a lead. He was never defensive. He'd go out there like Katy-bar-the-door and just attack and attack. He'd force you to gamble and try and catch him, and usually you'd make a mistake before he would."

7. The general who is skilled in defense hides in the most secret recesses of the earth; he who is skilled in attack flashes forth from the top-most heights of heaven. Thus on the one hand we have ability to protect ourselves; on the other, a victory that is complete.

One of the game's greatest golf course architects was Dr. Alister Mackenzie, who designed such magnificent courses as the Augusta National Golf Club, Cypress Point Golf Club, Royal Melbourne, and Lahinch.

Mackenzie served with the British army in the Boer War and made a careful study of camouflage. In fact, he was so impressed by the strategic effect of the Boers' camouflage that he wrote a magazine article praising the enemy for their imagination and expertise. His superiors considered court-martialing him. Eventually, cooler heads prevailed. Instead, they reduced his rank from major to lieutenant and ordered him to share his expertise with their own engineer corps. He incorporated what he learned into his designs, mentioning the principles of course design he developed in his classic text, *Golf Architecture,* that codified the thirteen features he felt comprised an ideal golf course. Using his knowledge of camouflage, he incorporated deception (not to be confused with trickery, however) in many of his designs, particularly when it came to protecting the putting surfaces from poorly conceived or badly executed approach shots.

Perfect examples of this deception are greens that are designed with a "false front." The front of the green slopes back towards the player, and while this might not be immediately detectable from back in the fairway, a shot that either fails to carry deep enough onto the putting surface or is hit with excessive spin runs the risk of rolling back off the green and onto the fairway. The ninth hole at Augusta National in an excellent example of a green that has a false front, and many a player over the years has counted a bogey, or worse, a penalty, for a misplayed approach on this hole.

Mackenzie is also widely praised for the natural appearance of his sand bunkers and other hazards.

"All artificial hazards should be made to fit into the ground as if placed there by nature," Mackenzie wrote.

Mackenzie realized that properly placed and designed bunkers, for example, presented more than just a strategic threat to a player. Such hazards effect a player's psychological approach by causing the element of doubt to enter into a player's thought process. This not only disrupts the ability to conceive the shot clearly, but can eliminate just enough confidence to affect the physical execution of the shot.

One of the best examples of this is the par-3 twelfth hole at Augusta National. The winds generally come down from the right, but then tend to swirl around as they pass over the elevated green. The difficulty in judging where the wind is as any given moment leads to confusion in a player's club selection, and can make it difficult for a player to completely commit to the shot he or she wants to hit. As a result, it is not uncommon for two players to hit the same club, only to look on in disbelief as one player's shot winds up short and in the water protecting the front of the green, while the second player's ball ends up in the back bunker—or worse.

Not for nothing has Jack Nicklaus called the twelfth at Augusta National, the "nastiest little par-3 in the world.

8. To see victory only when it is within the ken of the common herd is not the acme of excellence.

9. Neither is it the acme of excellence if you fight and conquer and the whole Empire says, "Well done!"

10. To lift an autumn hair is no sign of great strength; to see the sun and moon is no sign of sharp sight; to hear the noise of thunder is no sign of a quick ear.

Sun Tzu's point is that observing the obvious is not a mark of genius but being able to detect subtleties surely is.

Playing in the final round of the 1973 Masters Tournament, J. C. Snead was in the thick of the battle as he came to the difficult, par-3 twelfth hole. Number twelve is demanding for any variety of reasons. First of all, the green is very narrow and shots that aren't hit deep enough into the putting surface run the risk of rolling back into the pond that fronts the hole. Further complicating matters is the wind, which generally blows down the valley to the right of the hole and then swirls, making club selection extremely difficult.

Experienced players know that even if you feel the wind coming off your left shoulder on the tee, which is a helping wind, it might well be blowing from the right up at the green.

Snead was fooled by the wind and didn't take enough club. He wound up making a double-bogey five and finished second, one stroke behind Tommy Aaron.

11. What the ancients called a clever fighter is one who not only wins, but excels in winning with ease.

The late Dave Marr, who won three times on the PGA Tour including the 1965 PGA Championship,

knew just how hard it is to win at the highest levels of the game. That's why, as a golf analyst for ABC Sports, when he watched Amy Alcott win the 1980 U.S. Women's Open by nine strokes, he was suitably impressed.

"No one wins an Open by nine strokes," he said.

Sadly, Marr died in 1997 and never got a chance to watch Tiger Woods's remarkable—almost unbelievable—performance in the 2000 U.S. Open at the Pebble Beach Golf Links, when he won the championship by a staggering fifteen strokes, shooting a four-round score of 272, which tied the Open record set by Jack Nicklaus in 1980 at Baltusrol tied by Lee Janzen on the same course in 1998. His victory called to mind the 1977 British Open at Turnberry, when Tom Watson and Nicklaus blew away the rest of the field, turning the final thirty-six holes into essentially a match-play tournament between the two formidable champions. Watson wound up winning by a stroke.

"I figure I won the British Open," said Hubert Green, who finished a distant third. "I don't know what tournament those other two guys were playing."

12. Hence his victories bring him neither reputation for wisdom nor credit for courage.

In a perverse way, Sam Snead suffered from this fate. The beauty of his swing, his effortless power, his sublime short game and the man's feline grace made his victories seem absurdly easy.

One time Dave Marr, the respected golf analyst for ABC, NBC, and the BBC, was discussing different players he had known throughout his career.

"Rossie [Bob Rosburg, the winner of the 1959 PGA Championship] was the most natural golfer I ever saw," said Marr, who died in 1997 after a courageous battle with cancer.

"What about Sam Snead?" the writer asked.

"Sam doesn't count," said Marr. "He's supernatural."

Even people who should have known better occasionally discounted Snead's record.

For many years, *Golf Digest* gathered a group of outstanding players and teachers known as its "Pro Panel." The group would meet for three-day sessions to discuss a wide variety of subjects. One such discussion centered on great players. In the course of the session, Paul Runyan, a member of the World Golf Hall of Fame who won fifty tournaments including two PGA Championships, said that Snead was the "laziest great player he'd ever seen."

To his credit, he said it with Snead in the room.

To his credit, Snead acknowledged Runyan's right to his opinion.

Later, over dinner, Snead refuted Runyan's claim by pointing out that once, during an audit by the Internal Revenue Service, he produced documentation showing that in the course of his career, he'd hit millions of practice balls that somehow qualified as a business expense.

The auditor (who must have been a golfer) agreed, adding a new wrinkle to the history of tax law in the United States.

13. He wins his battles by making no mistakes. Making no mistakes is what establishes the certainty of victory, for it means conquering an enemy that is already defeated.

Simply put, golf is a game of minimizing your mistakes while waiting patiently for your opponent to make his own miscalculations or poorly played shots.

The best players are those that can read a golf course and figure where there is an opportunity to attack and have a good chance at making a birdie or better, and when discretion is the better part of valor.

One year, when playing the par-5 thirteenth at Augusta National, Ben Hogan elected to lay up short of the creek which protects the front of the putting surface. He went on to pitch onto the green, took two putts, and walked off with a carefully conceived and executed par.

After his round, an amateur who had played in the group behind Hogan, asked the great man why he elected to lay up when he certainly had enough length to reasonably expect to hit the green in two.

"Because I didn't need a three and I couldn't afford a six," was Hogan's terse and well-reasoned reply.

14. Hence the skillful fighter puts himself into a position which makes defeat impossible, and does not miss the moment for defeating the enemy.

Golf history is replete with examples of players hitting great shots at the moment when it can turn the momentum in their favor and puts them in position to score a victory. Surely one of the most momentous came in the final round of the 1960 U.S. Open at Cherry Hills Country Club near Denver.

In those days, "Open Saturday" consisted of thirty-six holes. After his morning round, Arnold Palmer was having lunch in the locker room and speaking with two writers, Dan Jenkins and the late Bob Drum. Palmer had won the Masters earlier in the year and was in position to win his first U.S. Open title if he could produce a great round in the afternoon.

The first hole at Cherry Hills is a short par-4.

Palmer thought that if could drive the green, it might get his round off to just the start he needed. That said, if his gamble failed and he drove into the deep rough, it might well end his chances.

"I'm going to drive that green this afternoon," he said.

"Good," said Drum, who had covered Palmer dating back to his days as an amateur in Pennsylvania. "Maybe you can finish twelfth."

This only kicked Palmer's already substantial competitive juices closer to a full boil.

"If I drive the first green and make a birdie or an eagle, maybe I can shoot a 65. That would give me 280 and doesn't 280 always win the Open?" Palmer asked.

"Yeah, when Hogan shoots it," said Jenkins.

Sufficiently inspired, Palmer went out, drove the green and two-putted for a birdie. Then he birdied the next three holes as well. After making a par on the fifth hole, he birdied numbers six and seven and took the lead, moving past the fourteen players that had been ahead of him on the scoreboard at the start of his round.

Palmer shot a 30 for the first nine than played the back nine in even par to post a 280 that gave him a two-stroke victory over a promising young amateur named Jack Nicklaus.

15. Thus it is that in war the victorious strategist only seeks battle after the victory has

been won, whereas he who is destined to defeat first fights and afterwards looks for victory.

The original *Shell's Wonderful World of Golf* series was one of the most popular golf shows ever televised. It featured the game's top players in head-to-head competition played at some of the world's finest courses.

The series, which ran from the early 1960s into the early 1970s, had any number of outstanding matches, but perhaps the greatest was one between Ben Hogan and Sam Snead played at the Houston Country Club.

While Snead had remained relatively active on Tour, Hogan had essentially retired from competitive golf, spending his time running his golf equipment company and playing golf socially with his friends in Fort Worth.

Once Hogan committed to playing, he went to work honing his game. He also arrived in Houston three days before the match and played several practice rounds, trying to determine the best way to approach each hole. Snead arrived just one day before the match and played one practice round.

While Snead played well, Hogan turned in a round that Gene Sarazen, who was working as a commentator for the series, called one of the greatest rounds he'd ever seen. Hogan hit every fairway and every green.

By taking the time to study the course and establish his strategy beforehand, Hogan exemplified the lesson Sun Tzu offers here.

16. The consummate leader cultivates the moral law, and strictly adheres to method and discipline; thus it is in his power to control success.

17. In respect of military method, we have, firstly, Measurement; secondly, Estimation of quantity; thirdly, Calculation; fourthly, Balancing of chances; fifthly, Victory.

18. Measurement owes its existence to Earth; Estimation of quantity to Measurement; Calculation to Estimation of quantity; Balancing of chances to Calculation; and Victory to Balancing of chances.

Few if any players ever prepared as diligently for a championship as Ben Hogan prepared for the 1953 British Open at Carnoustie, which had a justifiable reputation as one of the game's sternest tests.

Hogan had already won the 1953 Masters and U.S. Open, and while he had serious reservations about traveling to Scotland for the British Open, people he respected like Gene Sarazen and Tommy Armour prevailed on Hogan to at least play in the game's oldest championship one time.

Hogan and his wife, Valerie, arrived a week ahead of the tournament and he went to work, meticulously studying the course during a series of practice rounds. He would often play three balls from the tee, hitting a combination of fades and draws to see which left him the best approaches into Carnoustie's demanding greens. In addition, after dinner, he would return to the course, often walking the course in reverse to get a fresh perspective on the holes. He made note of distances, carefully studied the contours of the greens and the positioning of the bunkers. Carnoustie was unlike any course he had ever seen, and he wasn't entirely pleased by what he saw.

"The bunkers were put in there like a man throwing rice at a wedding," he said. "It looks like they just took a handful of bunkers and threw them out all over the course. I think they mow the greens once a week and the fairways once a month. I don't think they ever touch the rough. I've got a lawn mower back home in Texas. I think I'll send it over.

Hogan's comments did little to endear him to the locals, but they soon developing a grudging admiration for the man they came to call the "Wee Ice Mon."

In the end, Hogan's extraordinary preparation paid off handsomely. His score of 282 was four shots better than the best runners-up Frank Stranahan, Dai Rees, and Peter Thomson could manage and eight strokes better than any winning score in previous tournaments at Carnoustie. His final-round 68 set a course record.

"Hail to the greatest golfer of our time," wrote the respected Leonard Crawley in the London *Daily Telegraph.* "And who's to say he's not the greatest golfer of all time?"

19. A victorious army opposed to a routed one, is as a pound's weight placed in the scale against a single grain.

Or, in other words, nothing beats winning.

When Tom Kite won the 1992 U.S. Open at Pebble Beach Golf Links, he was forty-three years old and the victory was the seventeenth of a PGA Tour career that would help earn him induction into the World Golf Hall of Fame in 2004.

Kite would go on to win two more Tour events before shifting his focus to the Champions Tour, where he had posted seven victories coming into the 2006 season.

Shortly after his victory in the Open, he was talking with a writer and became philosophical on the subject of winning.

"The thing about winning the Open is that I did it at age forty-three," said Kite. "Any win is special, but to win at my age is extra-important because you never know if you last win is going to be your *last* win. If I had won the Open in my twenties or thirties, it would have been special, but I wonder if it would have been quite this special."

20. The onrush of a conquering force is like the bursting of pent-up waters into a chasm a thousand fathoms deep.

Momentum plays a crucial role in golf, particularly in match-play situations.

Going into the final day of the 1999 Ryder Cup, the United States team trailed the European side, 10–6.

When he was preparing his line-up for the singles play, the United States's captain, Ben Crenshaw, elected to put some of his strongest players out early. Tom Lehman, a former British Open champion (and captain of the 2006 U.S. Ryder Cup team) went off first, followed by Davis Love III, Phil Mickelson, Hal

Sutton, David Duval, Tiger Woods and Steve Pate. It proved to be a brilliant tactical move. The seven Americans swept their opponents, in some cases by wide margins. As the results were posted (to roars from the heavily pro-American galleries at The Country Club) the momentum shifted dramatically to the U.S. team, leaving the Europeans shaken and demoralized.

At the close of singles play, the United States had won 8½ points to the European's 3½. The result was enough to give the home team a 1-point victory.

CHAPTER V

Energy

1. Sun Tzu said: The control of a large force is the same principle as the control of a few men: it is merely a question of dividing up their numbers.

Jack Nicklaus didn't have to try and intimidate his fellow competitors. Just his presence was enough, particularly in the major championships. Curiously, the increased pressure of the majors benefited Nicklaus. In fact, Nicklaus always argued that the majors were easier for him to win than a weekly Tour event.

"When you come to a major, you can pretty

much eliminate half the field, maybe more," Nicklaus observed. "As you get to the final round, you can begin eliminating even more players, so in the end, there's really only a small percentage of the field that you're left to beat."

2. Fighting with a large army under your command is nowise different from fighting with a small one: it is merely a question of instituting signs and signals.

3. To ensure that your whole host may withstand the brunt of the enemy's attack and remain unshaken—this is affected by maneuvers direct and indirect.

4. That the impact of your army may be like a grindstone dashed against an egg—this is effected by the science of weak points and strong.

Byron Nelson was one of the most consistent players in the game's history. He was uncanny in his accuracy. In fact, even today Jack Nicklaus tells the story about the first time he ever saw Nelson in action.

"I was playing in the U.S. Junior Amateur and

Byron came and put on an exhibition," Nicklaus said. "They had just laid down the irrigation system and there was a line down the middle of the fairway where a pipe had been laid. Byron started with his short irons and worked his way through the bag until he was hitting his driver. The amazing thing is that ball after ball landed on that line, and those that didn't sure didn't miss by much."

Indeed, Nelson's play was so phenomenal that occasionally he would almost lose interest, which was the case in 1945 when he won eleven tournaments in a row and nineteen in all (eighteen of them official events). During his record run, the pressure ratcheted up from tournament to tournament.

"I just wish I would go out there and just blow up," Nelson told his wife, Louise, as he headed for the course one day.

When he returned home, Louise asked him if he'd blown up.

"Yes, I did," he said. "I shot a 68."

Years after Nelson's retirement, he was still held in awe by his fellow players.

"The man was just awesome in the way he'd just grind you down," said George Fazio. "When I had to play him I'd say, 'Oh, dear Lord, please get this over quick.' There was just no stopping him."

5. **In all fighting, the direct method may be used for joining battle, but indirect methods will be needed in order to secure victory.**

6. **Indirect tactics, efficiently applied, are inexhaustible as Heaven and Earth, unending as the flow of rivers and streams; like the sun and moon, they end but to begin anew; like the four seasons, they pass away to return once more.**

7. There are not more than five musical notes, yet the combinations of these five give rise to more melodies than can ever be heard.

Teaching professionals often stress the importance of proper fundamentals, especially when working with new golfers. There are several reasons for this. For starters, as a general rule in order to compensate for, say, a poor grip, it requires you to make an adjustment in some other part of your swing or in some other fundamental. Under the pressure of competition, that correction will almost certainly betray you.

But another important consideration is that proper fundaments make it possible for a player to learn a wide variety of shots—fades or draws, high shots or low—that can be used under any variety of circumstances. One of the all-time greatest in this department was Sam Snead. Even when he was well into his seventies, players would stop and watch him on the practice tee when he showed up at PGA Tour or Champions Tour events.

When Tom Kite turned professional and joined the Tour in the early 1970s, he received a great piece of advice from Bob Toski, one of the country's top teaching professionals and a former leading money-winner on Tour.

"When you get out on Tour, introduce yourself to Sam Snead the first chance you get," said Toski. "Ask if you can play practice rounds together. He'll want to play for a little cash but it will be the best investment you ever made."

Kite took Toski's advice and played numerous times with Snead. He came away suitably impressed and more than a little awed. When he returned home to Austin, he asked his longtime teacher, the sainted Harvey Penick, a simple question:

"Mr. Penick, do you think if a player worked really hard he could learn to hit the shots that Sam hits under pressure."

"Probably not," said Penick.

Snead had few rivals as a shotmaker, but one of them was Lee Trevino. If Snead had an edge over Trevino, it was in his ability to hit high, soft shots, whereas Trevino, because he had a relatively flat swing, had difficulty hitting similar shots. That was the main reason he felt that he was at such a disadvantage at Augusta National Golf Club.

"If you put me on the right type of course, like

a Donald Ross course, I will eat your lunch," Trevino explained. "I will eat your lunch every day. If we play four rounds I'm going to get you, because Donald Ross–type courses give me options. You can't put me in a position where I don't have an option. An option means that when I'm going into a green I can hit six different shots. If you put me in a position where I have to hit a 2-iron or a 4-wood into a green, I'm a dead man. Now, that's taking me out of my environment. When you put me a long, demanding golf course, I am totally dead. I can't play. But put me a course that lets me hit shots, and I can play with the best of them."

8. There are not more than five primary colors (blue, yellow, red, white, and black), yet in combination they produce more hues than can ever been seen.

Today's golfers are fortunate enough to be playing in a second golden era of course design. The first featured creations by the likes of Donald Ross, Dr. Alister Mackenzie, C. B. McDonald, A. W. Tillinghast and the like. Today's architects schooled themselves on the works of these masters and then added the benefits of modern education and sophisticated technology.

It is said that all golf course architecture is rooted in the game's most famous course, the Old Course at St. Andrews, which is a product of evolution as much as a grand design. In fact, for much of its history the course played in a clockwise rather than the current counterclockwise fashion. It has numerous double greens, a seemingly endless number of bunkers, many quite severe and penal, and rolling, undulating fairways which, when firm and fast as they should be, create all sorts of bounces—both good and bad, expected and surprising. Unlike so many modern courses which take advantage of water hazards, water only comes into play on the first hole and only then if the approach to the green is very poorly played.

The Old Course does not automatically inspire feelings of love at first sight. In fact, players quite often have just the opposite reaction.

Sam Snead arrived by train for the 1946 British Open. As the train pulled into St. Andrews at dusk, he looked out the window and commented to one of his fellow travelers, "Look yonder at that farm there. It looks like an old golf course that's gone to seed."

Wars have been started for less.

Five-time British Open champion Peter Thomson, perhaps the game's most eloquent proponent of links golf, had a similar reaction to the Old Course but quickly came to love the course and the cerebral challenge it presented. For more than anything else, the Old Course is the ultimate strategic test, requiring players to hit their drives in precisely the right part of the fairway in order to avail a player the best angle for the approach shot. And because St. Andrews sits hard by the North Sea, the constantly shifting winds can dramatically alter how the course plays, often several times in the course of a round.

It is not surprising, therefore, that when Bobby Jones and Dr. Alister MacKenzie collaborated on their design for the Augusta National Golf Club their labors were done with the Old Course in mind. The idea was to replicate the strategic demands and shot values presented by the Old Course but present them in a parkland setting—an audacious challenge that they met supremely well.

Jones did not immediately recognize the considerable charms of the Old Course. In fact, his first visit there, for the 1921 British Open, prompted a humiliating display of temper that he regretted for the rest of his life.

Playing the par-3 eleventh hole in the third round, he made a 6, tore up his scorecard, and walked off the course, prompting the wrath and scorn of the assembled writers and officials.

Still, he came to love the course and, indeed, the town itself.

"The more I studied the Old Course the more I loved it, and the more I loved it the more I studied it, so that I came to feel that it was for me the most favorable meeting ground possible for an important contest," he said. "I felt that my knowledge of the course enabled me to play it with patience and restraint until she might exact her toll from my adversary, who might treat her with less respect and understanding."

Until the end of his life, Jones kept a line drawing of the Old Course in his office.

One of the best descriptions of the variety and challenges presented by a talented architect came from A. W. Tillinghast in his description of the courses he designed at Winged Foot.

"As the various holes came to life, they were of a sturdy breed," Tillinghast wrote. "The contouring of the greens places a premium on the placement of drives, but never is there a necessity of facing a prodigious carry of the sink-or-swim sort. It is only the knowledge that the next shot is to be played with rifle accuracy that brings the realization that the drive must be placed precisely. The holes are like men, all rather similar from foot to neck, but with the greens showing the same varying character as human faces."

No architect ever received greater acclaim for his putting surfaces than Donald Ross, not only for the greens themselves, but the challenges they presented for golfers whose approaches either missed or failed to remain on them. His masterpiece, Pinehurst Number Two in Pinehurst, North Carolina, is the textbook example of what this dictum from Sun Tzu is referring to as it pertains to the short game.

Like Tillinghast, Ross believed a well-designed hole should place a premium on the approach shot. One that is precisely conceived and executed should be rewarded, while those lacking in those equalities should be punished commensurate to the degree of error.

When the United States Golf Association brought the U.S. Open to Pinehurst Number Two in 1992, it marked a decided change in their traditional philosophy of course setup for the national championship. As a general rule, U.S. Open courses feature narrow fairways lined with deep, thick rough. Ideally, the fairways and greens are firm and fast, the better to punish errant shots. Critics of the USGA, however, argued that by protecting the greens with penal rough, it negated the advantage players with exceptional short games might enjoy. In short, if you missed a green, you were at the mercy of luck more than sheer skill and nerve.

All that changed at Number Two. Balls that failed to stay on the crowned greens Ross favored often ran down into swales and unless the shot was very badly misplayed—or the player got a really bad break—the ball came to rest on short grass.

Ah, but that's when things got interesting, as well as frustrating and, in some cases, maddening. The beauty of Ross's handiwork is that it gave the players a staggering and even paralyzing series of options. Players could hit high pitches, subtle chips, pitch and runs, or even putt the ball, taking spin out of play. The end result of all this was that a great many players suffered from a great deal of indecision, which was reflected in the scoring. On a course without a real water hazard, and rough that was relatively moderate, Payne Stewart's wining score of one-under-par 279 was the only sub-par total.

It is also worth noting that the USGA's averred goal of "identifying the best players in the game" had produced a champion that was, indeed, one of the top players in the world, but a runner-up that was equally celebrated—Phil Mickelson. The two had a lot in common, not the least of which were brilliant short games.

Just as Donald Ross's designs embodied this observation from Sun Tzu, so did the work of Robert Trent Jones, the man who can fairly be called the father of modern golf course architecture.

Jones was really the first designer to make use of water hazards on a spectacular scale. This was due, in part, because improvements in golf course irrigation systems made it preferable for courses to have their own generous and inexpensive water supplies, which usually meant ponds. Jones reasoned that if a course needed to have ponds, than why not bring them into play.

When working with Bobby Jones to design the Peachtree Golf Club in Atlanta, the two men discussed the merits of water hazards versus sand bunkers.

"Trent," the great amateur said. "What you have to bear in mind is that the difference between a sand bunker and a water hazard is the same difference between a car wreck and a plane crash. You might survive a car accident but a plane crash is a far more serious matter."

Jones took that to heart, and it greatly influenced what became known as his "heroic" design strategy.

Jones believed that a key to a great hole is that it clearly presents players with a series of options, ranging from the safe and conservative to the risky and daring. This theory of "risk-reward" design holds that a player has a choice—based on his confidence and skill level—to gamble and try to make a birdie or even an eagle, or have the option of playing safe and avoiding a bogey or worse.

The textbook example of this is his work on the

East Course at Dorado Beach in Puerto Rico and, more precisely, the 550-yard, par-5 thirteenth hole, one of Jones's favorites.

The hole is a double dogleg that turns twice around water hazards. Players must decide how much of the first dogleg they dare to cut off from the tee and then, face another decision for their second shot, when they can gamble and try to reach the green in two, or play safe and shoot for the green with a short iron on their third shot.

"The hole is fair to all players, no matter how skilled," Jones observed. "It is demanding, to be sure, but it demonstrates clearly all the rewards and penalties that should be innate to all great golf holes."

9. There are not more than five cardinal tastes (sour, acrid, salt, sweet, bitter), yet combinations of them yield more flavors than can ever be tasted.

Today's golfers have an enormous advantage when it comes to equipment. Today's technology offers a seemingly endless combination of components that can be precisely matched to a player's body type and swing shape. In addition, balls come in a staggering variety of designs that can also be precisely fitted to a player's needs.

This is far from the way things were even a decade or two ago, let alone back in the days of hickory shafts and balls that were out-of-round or otherwise defective more often than they were perfect.

A few years ago, Frank Thomas, who had overseen equipment testing for the United States Golf Association, tested a dozen MacGregor Tourney golf balls, the same type of ball used by Jack Nicklaus at the height of his career. Thomas's verdict was that, compared to today's balls, the Tourney balls were almost unplayable, which led Thomas to ponder how many more tournaments Nicklaus might have won if he'd played a better ball.

It's not only the balls that have dramatically improved in recent years. Clubs are also infinitely better.

Back in the 1980s, frequency matching was introduced. This was a way to check the relative flex and kick points of shafts within a set of clubs. Tom Weiskopf, the winner of the 1973 British Open, had played with the same MacGregor irons throughout his career. One day he decided to have the shafts checked. The results showed that all the shafts in his irons were remarkable similar except for one.

"That club always felt a little funny to me," said Weiskopf. "I had to make a different swing with it."

10. In battle, there are not more than two methods of attack—the direct and the indirect; yet these two in combination give rise to an endless series of maneuvers.

As applied to golf, this speaks directly to how a player decides to play a hole. You can directly attack it with a bold, decisive play and run the risks inherent in that decision, or you can take a more circumspect approach and play it indirectly, settling for par but generally avoiding any costly mistakes.

Perhaps the best example of a hole that offers this strategic decision is the "Road Hole" at the Old Course at St. Andrews.

The seventeenth is a par-4 that presents a challenge to players off the tee. The hole is a sharp dogleg to the right, and players have the option if driving over the dogleg which, if successful, can cut substantial yardage off the second shot but also brings the out-of-bounds into play.

Part of the appeal for cutting over the dogleg is that the green is one of the most intimidating in the game. The left front of the putting surface is guarded by a fearsome bunker, but shots that carry over the green run the risk of either coming to rest on the adjacent road (hence the name of the hole) or against a stone wall. Both are in play.

Playing Cyril Tolley in the fourth round of the 1930 British Amateur, Bobby Jones found himself tied in what had been an extremely close match, as both players held one-up leads three different times.

Both players elected to drive over the corner and Jones was away. As he studied his shot, it occurred to him that the safest place to aim his approach was to the left of the green. He had never seen anyone deliberately hit a shot there, but he decided that if he was going to miss the green (he was wise enough not to even think about shooting at the flagstick) than this was the safest play.

Jones's ball hit a spectator, but as luck would have it, it came to rest just where Jones had hoped. It left him a clear shot to the hole. For his part, Tolley aimed towards the right of the green, but ended up just short of the bunker—a very lucky break, indeed.

Jones pitched to within eight feet and made the putt, his indirect approach rewarded. Only a miraculous pitch to with two feet of the hole by Tolley (who called it the finest shot of his career) allowed him to halve Jones, who went on to win the championship on the first hole of a sudden-death playoff.

11. The direct and the indirect lead on to each other in turn. It is like moving in a circle—you never come to an end. Who can exhaust the possibilities of their combination?

Again, so much in a round of golf is fluid. Momentum shifts in a round, as does a player's strength and confidence. For example, the shots you might be able to play early in a round, when your strength and energy levels are high, may be more difficult in the closing holes. This is also a matter of confidence. If you are playing well and thinking clearly, it is far more likely that you will have fewer doubts and suffer less from indecision than if you hit a rocky patch in a round and are struggling. In addition, there are holes that can be attacked and those that must be played conservatively, although this may change as the complexion of a match of tournament shifts. The thrust of Sun Tzu's point here is that while it is important to have a carefully conceived course strategy, it is equally important to be flexible in the face of changing conditions. There is also the important consideration of shifts in the weather. A change in the strength of direction of the wind can make a course play entirely different. This is particularly true on a seaside layout like the Old Course at St. Andrews, where the winds play such a dominant and important part in course management. You will come to appreciate this if you watch the Masters Tournament. Commentators will often talk about the wind direction, since it can completely alter how a hole plays, particularly the holes on the back nine, where the winds tend to sweep down through the treelined fairways and then swirl around the greens, creating confusion, indecision, and frequently, errors in judgment and execution, even by players with years of experience playing Augusta National.

Acknowledgments

R ight from the start, I want to thank two extraordinary gentlemen, Jofie Ferrari-Adler and John Oakes.

A couple years ago, Jofie proposed that I do a book of stories and anecdotes based on golf gambling. While my only experience in the subject stemmed from having the most expensive six-handicap in North America, we went ahead with *Wanna Bet?* It was a lot of fun and, happily, very successful.

Shortly after its publication, Jofie called and asked if I'd ever heard of Sun Tzu's *The Art of War.* When I admitted that I hadn't a clue what he was talking about, he gave me a quick overview and sent out a copy of Sun Tzu's masterpiece, as well as books applying it to poker and business management—two other subjects where I am woefully lacking in knowledge or experience (or interest, for that matter).

At any rate, I quickly came to see how many of Sun Tzu dictums could be applied to golf and off we went to work on *Golf and the Art of War*.

Shortly thereafter, Jofie took a position with another publishing house and John Oakes, a vice president of Avalon and the publisher of Avalon imprints Thunder's Mouth Press and Nation Books, took over the project. Like Jofie, he has been a joy to work with—patient, encouraging, and enthusiastic. To the extent that *Golf and the Art of War* is successful, these two guys deserve a lot of the credit.

My agent, Tara Mark at RLR and Associates also deserves a nod. Her support and wise counsel are invaluable and deeply appreciated. She is taking up golf, which is something of a surprise—I would have thought that representing me was punishment enough.

Finally, thanks to my wife, Julia, and our kids, Ben, Darcy, and Andy. Without their love and support, I would have to get a real job.